THE HOPI PHOTOGRAPHS
KATE CORY: 1905-1912

Library of Congress Cataloging-in-Publication Data

Cory, Kate, 1861–1958.
The Hopi photographs.

Reprint. Originally published: La Cañada, Calif. : Chaco Press, c1986.
"Kate Cory : artist of Arizona / [by] Marnie Gaede;
A Hopi essay, captions & quotes / [by] Barton Wright;
photographic reproductions / [by] Marc Gaede."
Bibliography: p.
1. Hopi Indians—Pictorial works.
2. Cory, Kate, 1861–1958.
I. Gaede, Marnie.
II. Wright, Barton.
III. Gaede, Marc.
IV. Title.
E99.H7C63   1988   779′.9979100497   87-34261
ISBN 0-8263-1058-3
ISBN 0-8263-1059-1 (pbk.)

THE HOPI PHOTOGRAPHS

KATE CORY: 1905-1912

Copyright © 1986 by Chaco Press.
All rights reserved.
University of New Mexico Press edition reprinted 1988 by
arrangement with Chaco Press.

THE HOPI PHOTOGRAPHS
KATE CORY: 1905-1912

KATE CORY: ARTIST OF ARIZONA
MARNIE GAEDE

A HOPI ESSAY, CAPTIONS & QUOTES
BARTON WRIGHT

PHOTOGRAPHIC REPRODUCTIONS
MARC GAEDE

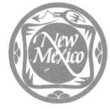

UNIVERSITY OF NEW MEXICO PRESS
ALBUQUERQUE

"That is my home." She murmured the words lovingly, her gaze noting the uneven line the falling stone houses made against the blue sky. "Yes," she thought, "in that place of ruins is the evidence of my beginnings. My roots are there. A part of me is there still, in the old home of my parents, in the hill house of my grandmother, in the very dust that whispers in the streets where I played so long ago. Is that where I belong, now?"

No Turning Back
POLINGAYSI QOYAWAYMA (ELIZABETH Q. WHITE).
UNIVERSITY OF NEW MEXICO PRESS, ALBUQUERQUE. 1964.

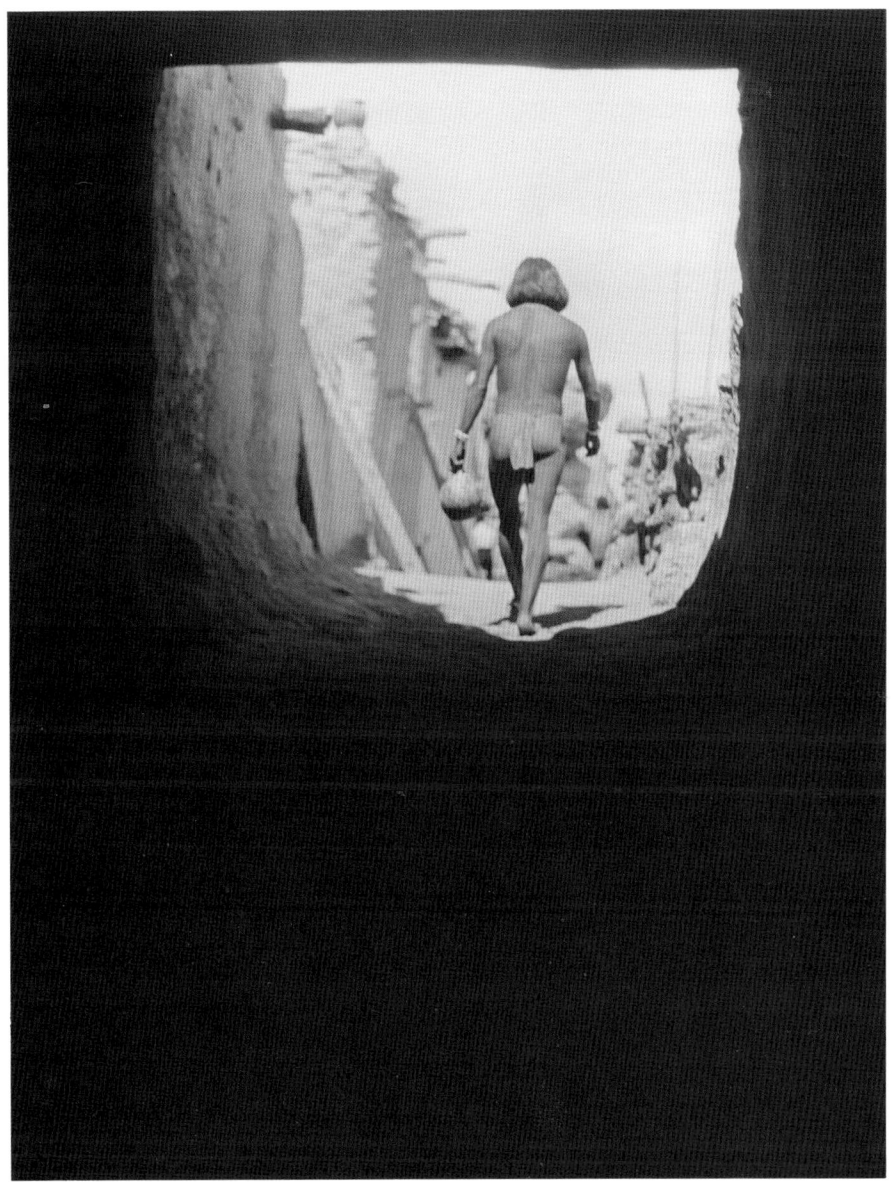

Kutka, carrying a canteen, passes through the kiskya and down the south side of Walpi.

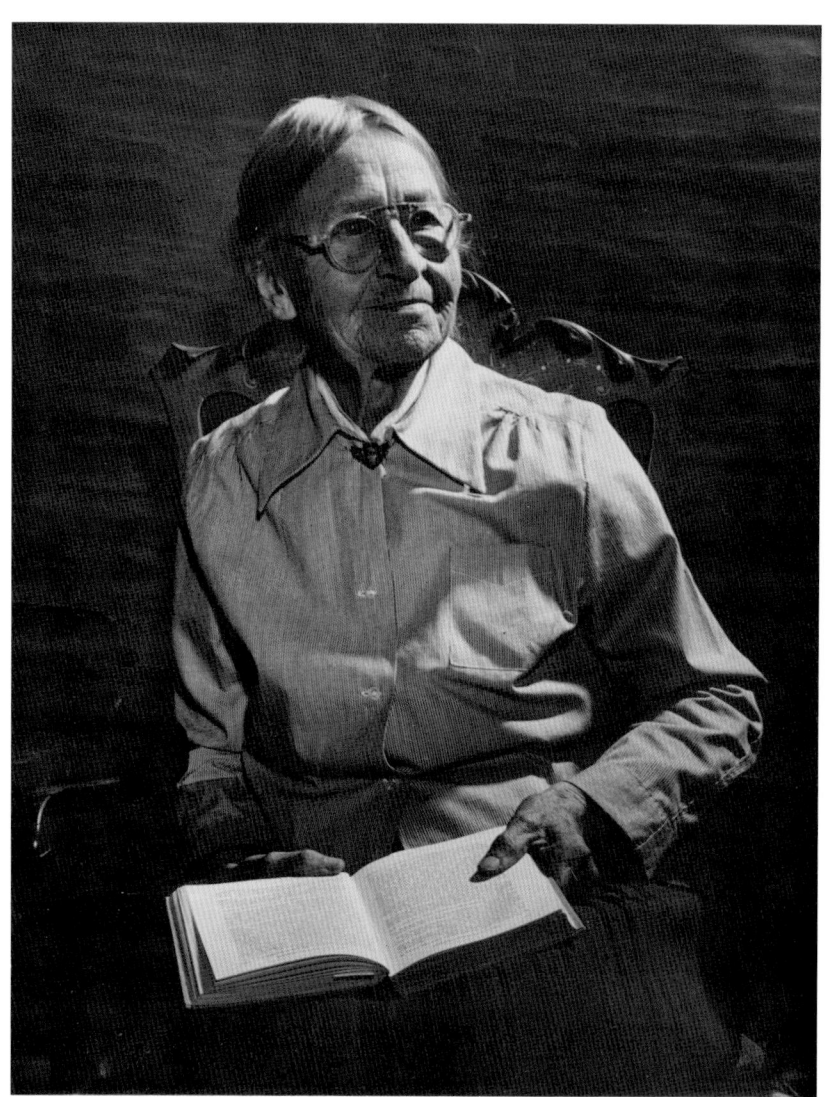
Kate Thompson Cory. Portrait circa 1951 by Charles Troncy.

KATE CORY: ARTIST OF ARIZONA

On a torrid afternoon in 1905 a train rumbling through the Arizona Territory suddenly stopped at Canyon Diablo, in the middle of nowhere. A porter jumped down, unloaded some luggage, and the train pulled away, leaving a single passenger—Kate Thompson Cory—standing in the hot, gritty wind. She shielded her eyes against the glare of the sun and watched her link with civilization roll out of sight. When it was gone she lowered her hand. Above her a hawk banked on a thermal. Something yapped in a canyon. Antelope studied her from a barren ridge, ready to run. She had an anxious moment then, but it passed. After all, if things didn't work out she would simply present her ticket, go back to New York City and continue the pleasant, uneventful life well-bred ladies of her era were encouraged to lead.

Not much is known about Kate Cory's earlier years. She was born February 8, 1861, in Waukegan, Illinois. Her father, James Y. Cory, was the editor of the Waukegan *Weekly Gazette*. A crusading Abolitionist and an organizer of the Underground Railroad, he came to the attention of Abraham Lincoln, and they soon became friends. She received an art education at Cooper Union and the Art Student's League in New York City. She never married. We must assume that she made art during this period, but none of her work has survived.

In 1904 she attended a social gathering of the Pen and Brush Club, an organization of New York artists. She was introduced to Louis Akin, a painter who had just returned from a year of work on the Hopi mesas of northern Arizona. It didn't take long for Akin, ecstatic about the beauty and the strange Indian culture he had found there, to convince her that it was a perfect place to start an artist colony.

Although Akin's dream didn't come true, Kate Cory never used that return ticket to New York. She couldn't have known it at the time, but the moment she entered Arizona the adventure of her life began. She would find in the Southwest whatever it was she couldn't get in New York. And in the process become one of the very few outsiders ever allowed to look into the heart of Hopi life.

The extraordinary photographs on these pages are a result of that trust. Chosen for their aesthetic and historic importance, they were culled from 642 negatives remaining of the group Cory took in the seven years she lived at the Hopi villages of Oraibi and Walpi, from 1905 to 1912. This collection has never been published before. We have ordered the images according to the Hopi ceremonial calendar, and located descriptions of the scenes they portray from the library of books and articles written about the Hopi since 1776. What Cory has shown us is not only the rhythms of the Hopi day, but social and sacred events never before seen through the lens of a camera. Some of these images are the only visual record of exotic customs which the Hopi no longer practice.

The physical hardships she had to endure at Walpi were enormous. She could have chosen to live in the style of the few whites who had settled in the area, but she preferred to be close to the Indians. Why they accepted her with such grace is a mystery. The Hopi are profoundly suspicious of outsiders, a facet of their culture resulting from centuries of attempted political and religious suppression by the Spanish, other tribes, and finally by the U.S. But not only did the women welcome Cory into their daily lives, the men—who excluded even Hopi women from much of the religious life of the mesas—invited her into the kivas. This intimacy is apparent in her work.

That she could have achieved such high technical quality in her images is equally remarkable. She became an adept and dextrous photographer at a time when most Americans considered the medium a novelty. And not only was she working in isolation, denied the opportunity to compare notes with colleagues, her access to equipment and supplies was limited. Once her negatives were exposed, she developed them in a primitive darkroom at Walpi using rainwater from which she often had to extract dead rodents before it could be strained. Many of her first efforts were technically crude, but two of the images reproduced here stand out. PLATE 46 is the only known documentation of the violence that flared during the fierce and historically significant split between Oraibians in 1906; PLATE 47 is perhaps the finest early photograph ever taken of the Hopi village of Oraibi.

Cory, through trial and error, finally mastered the medium. The tonal quality in her later work is very high, and could only have been achieved through careful exposure and development. Also, it's clear that she discovered the secrets of focusing —her pictures became sharp corner-to-corner. The film speed at that time was quite slow, yet her images of certain religious ceremonies observed at dawn and dusk are sharp, indicating that she mounted her camera on a tripod. The spontaneity of some other photos demonstrate that she also learned how to *hold* the camera with a knowing hand.

Since photographic collections of the Hopi are rare, it's easy to compare Kate Cory's with the others. A collection of Pueblo photos executed by Edward S. Curtis comes to mind immediately. Curtis customarily arrived at the mesas before a photography session with a wagonload of cultural finery. Then, when his subjects were dressed to the teeth, he posed them. As a result, his photographs look affected and unnatural in the sentimental style of the period. Cory's camera was a quiet presence that recorded people as they really were, dressed in the simple clothing they wore every day. Because Curtis was attempting to document every tribe in the U.S., he could only spare enough time to show up at the Hopi mesas on ceremonial occasions in fair weather. Cory lived with her subjects, knew them by name, experienced their joy and grief, their births and their deaths, their happiness when it rained, their fear of drought, the heat and the cold they endured. Her understanding and admiration for them informs every photograph.

Other photographers had been to Hopi before Cory. The most notable of these was Adam Clark Vroman, whose recently published collection was made between 1895 and 1902. Vroman was a thorough professional who used glass plate negatives and large view cameras. The clarity of his images is excellent, but they display a certain contrivance that's unavoidable when subjects are conscious of the photographer. Jo Mora, whose images form the only other collection besides Cory's that spans the ceremonial calendar, visited the Hopi from time to time between 1903 and 1912. But his photographs are mostly documentative, lacking the sensitivity and eye for composition that make Cory's images special. After 1912 few interesting photographs were taken at Hopi. After 1917 there were none. That was the year the Hopi—one of the most unique and most studied cultures in the world—finally got tired of the relentless scrutiny of outsiders and banned photographers from the mesas. To this day, woe be to him who tries to sneak a camera into one of their villages.

Although the ban protected Hopi privacy it also made it difficult to keep a complete record of the past. Before the discovery of the Cory collection, in fact, it was thought that the conduct and design of certain discarded rites and ceremonies she photographed had died with the old priests. We hope her photographs can be useful to those Hopi whose interest in the old ways has recently been revived.

As illuminating as Cory's photographs are, it must be remembered that she came to the Southwest to paint, and that much of her life was spent doing just that. Among the places her paintings are displayed is the Smoki Museum in Prescott, Arizona, and at the Smithsonian Institution in Washington. Only a couple of her friends knew anything about her efforts as a photographer. It was not something she talked about. Maybe she used her camera to record images she would later attempt to render on canvas; maybe she was actually trying to train herself to be a professional photographer and felt dissatisfied with her progress. We can only guess.

Cory also wrote about the Hopi, publishing articles in a now defunct magazine called *The Border*. And she applied her untrained skills as an anthropological observer to record what she could of Hopi culture. She left behind a diary of events from the years 1907 and 1908, and a dictionary of the difficult Hopi tongue, along with the negatives reproduced here. Although she was an amateur linguist and her pronunciation renditions are imprecise, Cory's investigations are—along with those of Henry R. Voth —the first documentation of the language.

At the age of fifty-one, for unknown reasons, Cory left the mesas. She eventually settled in Prescott and spent the rest of her life there. She built her own home, but never got around to finishing the inside. The house was always cluttered with books, paintings and works in progress. She unexplainably had the doors installed upside down so the knobs would be too high for children to reach. She shunned most modern appliances and did her cooking on an aging wood stove. She was a vegetarian, dressed in long tattered skirts with ruffles, wore her hair in a bun and rarely accepted social invitations, although she occasionally asked people into her home. Some of her Prescott friends recall a day when the Hopi came to visit. Cory was showing them gifts various Arizona tribes had given her, when their attention riveted on one artifact in particular. It was an old digging stick that turned out to be an important icon representing crop fertility long sought by the Hopi Cloud Clan. They were ecstatic when she returned it to them. Once it was put back in its proper place in the fields, it could be beneficial again.

How Cory supported herself the last half of her life is a puzzle. She sold a few of her paintings to neighbors and a few to buyers. The prices she charged were low and it's doubtful she made a living from them. Her friends assumed she received trust money from back East but money was another subject she didn't talk about. We do know that one of her relatives, a man who had moved to Prescott for his tuberculosis, left her an insurance settlement when he died. Her clothes were so ragged that fellow members of the Congregational Church let the pastor know they were willing to buy her new clothes. Because she was so thin people thought she couldn't afford to buy food. Yet she gave away money to people she thought needed it more. In one case, she gave away a house and a lot to a man and his bride.

She was considered a congenial, generous eccentric and a very poor businesswoman by those who didn't know her. Those who knew her loved her. In her last years frailty forced her to move into the Pioneer's Home in Prescott, where she died on June 12, 1958 at the age of ninety-seven. She was buried on a knoll overlooking town under a granite tombstone with a bronze plaque that reads: *"Kate Cory, Artist of Arizona. Hers was the joy of giving."*

—MARNIE GAEDE

A HOPI ESSAY

Bounded by the sweeping curve of the Little Colorado, the high desert mesas of northeastern Arizona jut southwesterly; rocky fingers in a sea of sand reaching for the distant blue snow-capped mountains. Flat topped ridges with sides slowly crumbling and scattered small junipers hunched into the sandy slopes, it seems a sterile and inhospitable land. Yet the Hopi people who claim this marginal world occupied it by choice nearly one thousand years ago. They were not misguided, for the barren rocky summits collect the scarce rainfall and the sandy reaches horde the water, allowing it to drain slowly away into the springs at the base of the cliffs. Down the flat valleys between the mesas rush the flood waters of summer thunderstorms to irrigate and occasionally drown the fields of corn. Carefully used, the moisture is adequate for the needs of the people and their farming. Generation following generation refined their knowledge of where and how to plant and wove a blanket of tradition to protect the use of the land. Always balanced between drought and adequacy, the need of water fostered and encouraged a religion which strengthened and aided the Hopi, a bulwark against adversity. This religion peopled the land with spirits who rode the skies as clouds, drifted with the snows and fogs of winter, the mists from the springs, and in the water itself. Demi-deities represented the essence of rocks, the land, trees, stars, and snakes, and all other manner of things. These supernaturals possessed qualities and powers the opposite of Man's, who could be dealt with through the medium of ritual. Reasonable inhabitants of an "Other World," they would trade rain for the soft breast feathers of eagles and remain near the bright and happy dances of the people.

Into this well-balanced and ordered life came the first European intruders over four hundred years ago. They came seeking gold and souls to save. They came first in driblets and then in streams to batter at the beliefs of the Hopi, but like the mesas they inhabit the Hopi are an indomitable race so the tide receded leaving only a slight residue. But the movement and impact of the Spanish effort had far-reaching effects. Dislocated and disrupted tribes along the Rio Grande who collided with one another and reshuffled as they strove for balance, presented the Hopi with a new problem. The Navajo moved westward among the Hopi. Unwelcome people, both they and the Apache stole the fruits of the year's labor and disrupted the age-old patterns of farming. As the Hopi attempted to overcome this difficulty they were beset anew by an even more ruthless enemy who appeared in the guise of a friend. A new nation, scarcely more than fifty years old, the United States of America flexed its muscles and moved westward first touching the lives of the Hopi lightly. But as the contacts continued to increase the requests for assistance became demands that the Hopi abandon their centuries-old ways and change to fit a pattern conceived within the lifetime of one man. Hopi resistance was not hostile but rather a grim clinging to their own land and well-learned ways of farming with its all pervasive religious beliefs.

Possibly it was the attraction of an embattled people living in a starkly beautiful world that brought the burgeoning horde of explorers, scientists, and later tourists, to their land. More probably it was Hopi religion expressed in dance and ceremony, that has been the lure that has drawn countless thousands to this land. It has drawn them for a variety of reasons, to attempt its disruption, to record and study, or merely to enjoy and appreciate the beauty and drama of the dances much as the old Hopi spirits were drawn to the same ceremonies. Missionaries and sea captains, ethnologists and archaeologists, doctors and artists, came trooping, impelled often by curiosity and then entrapped to return again and again. Kate Cory, a woman living before her time, an artist and individualist, was one of these. Not content with an occasional passive observation, she flung herself fresh from the East, into the ancient provinciality of Walpi. Living with these hospitable people, she glimpsed more than all but a mere handful of outsiders, the essence of the Hopi. It is unclear whether she photographed to help in her painting or whether she recorded the Hopi to help her remember them. Certainly her paintings do not reflect the total involvement that the photographs express. Regardless of the reason, we remain forever in her debt, for she left an invaluable record not only for us but for the Hopi as well. The photographs are a moment frozen in time, when change had not yet overwhelmed the enduring Hopi. It seems only reasonable that Kate Cory's photographs reflect the views of those who also shared with her a kinship or understanding of the Hopi just as her photographs illustrate what the others saw. Hence the statements of travelers, authors, scientists, and the Hopi themselves coupled with the photographs become a composite statement about a remarkable people.

—BARTON WRIGHT

PRINTING THE KATE CORY IMAGES

Although Kate Cory probably realized the importance of making fine prints, the absence of the necessary darkroom equipment and material available at the turn of the century in the Southwest precluded any such endeavor. As a result, there are few original prints from this collection, and none of publishable quality. The negatives, however, keep the information exposed on them and we made new prints from these for reproduction. Because of the overwhelming superiority in the quality of modern lenses, general equipment, chemistry, and emulsions, it is safe to say that Cory never realized the full potential of her negatives. We made every effort to ensure that the undiminished beauty of her images was reproduced.

All prints were made on a standard 4 × 5 enlarger, fitted with a coldlight projection source. The developer was Beers Two-Solution with sodium carbonate substituted for potassium carbonate. The restrainer was benzotriazole used in amounts to permit full development but not to adversely affect the print tone. Most of the prints were subject to reduction so as to clear the highlights and add to the general brilliance of the image. The reducer was a Ferricyanide-Thiocyanate combination of considerable strength. Chlorobromide paper was exclusively utilized, and all prints were slightly toned in selenium.

In making the reproduction images, a print of medium contrast was desired. This was done so as to allow the fullest range of tones in the printers ink. The black and white image inherently gains contrast in both the half-tone and the duo-tone printing process. If the upper and lower values are important, then one has to make a slightly subdued print for the photolithographer. Moreover, the contrast can be expanded by extending the photolithography development process, which can reproduce the original brilliance of a salon quality print. To achieve the uniformity and desired quality, it is mandatory the photographer work closely with the photolithographer.

This technique, so successfully developed by Ansel Adams prior to the laser beam photolithography process, is what we applied to the reproduction of these photographs. The highly acclaimed laser beam procedure does achieve the highest level of brilliance, and in some cases a more interesting image than the original. But we believe it can also create a monotonous continuum. After viewing many such images in succession, an undesirable uniformity becomes apparent and the photographs take on a factory made, rather than a handcrafted quality.

The Kate Cory negatives were all made between 1905 and 1912 on nitro-cellulose film. In addition to the unstable nitrate film, the negatives were carelessly stored, which resulted in further deterioration of the images. Most of the prints had over four hundred spots and scratches that had to be removed, requiring exceptional amounts of time and patience. Some had over a thousand, a few over five thousand, and one had almost ten thousand. The negatives were conserved through the processes of refixing and washing, risky procedures regardless of the caution exercised. All but one of the Cory images survived, however. When we got to Plate 19, the Velvet Shirt Kachinas, the entire emulsion separated from its base. Because of the mucous-like quality of the emulsion, we were forced to print the image "wet," through a thin bath of water.

Few liberties were taken in the cropping of the negatives. Cory was a painter and her skill in composition left little to be improved upon. What changes were made correspond to her intent, with an understanding of the limitations to the situation and of the type of photography in which she was engaged.

At this time, nothing remains of the collection, except the negatives and a handful of contact prints, to testify to the actual photographic techniques and equipment used by Cory. But such information is of small consequence when compared to the beauty of the images and what they portray. —MARC GAEDE

LIST OF PLATES

1. Ahül completes his call at the Mong Kiva in Walpi.
2. Chief from the Chivato Kiva waits for Ahül to complete his call to the sun.
3. Ahül passing through the village pausing to mark the houses.
4. Pachavu procession moves up the southwest slope of Old Oraibi.
5. Eototo and Aholi address their attention to the cloud symbol on the ground at Oraibi.
6. Crow Mother prepares to enter a kiva with two Whipper Kachinas.
7. Nataska Kachinas stamp and growl before a house in Sichomovi.
8. Heheya Kachina receives a dish of corn flour from the occupant of a house at First Mesa.
9. A young Hopi maiden ceremonially dressed, contemplates the valley below her.
10. A young Hopi girl wearing the traditional butterfly hair whorls and maiden shawl.
11. From the kiskya, a Hopi girl looks across the valley of Polacca Wash at Walpi.
12. A Hopi man carries a dead infant to the cemetery.
13. A line of Anak'china enter the plaza at Sichomovi.
14. A group of Hopi mock their Navajo neighbors with the antics of the Tasavu clowns in the plaza at Shipaulovi.
15. A single Ma-alo Kachina dances on the rooftops of Walpi.
16. A line of Chakwaina Kachinas move into position at Oraibi.
17. Kachina dancers eat and rest below the cliffs at Walpi.
18. Members of a Mixed Kachina dance pause to rest at First Mesa.
19. A line of Velvet Shirt Kachinas move across the plaza at Walpi.
20. Two couples perform the Buffalo dance in the plaza at Walpi.
21. Supela of Walpi.
22. Wiki, Antelope priest of Walpi.
23. Kutka of Walpi sits spinning yarn.
24. A Hopi man sits weaving a blanket.
25. An elderly woman trudges through Kiakochomovi with a load of wood upon her back.
26. Portrait of a Tewa man.
27. A Hopi woman carries water to her home in Sichomovi.
28. A young married woman with corn flour on her face in traditional dress.
29. Hopi portrait.
30. Hopi portrait.
31. A Hopi man gathers his corn.
32. A bountiful crop of corn covers the rooftops of Walpi.
33. Women and young children string corn at First Mesa.
34. A Hopi woman shelling corn.
35. A Hopi woman making piki.
36. A Navajo woman attends a Hopi horse race.
37. Two young Hopi horsemen.

38. Niman Kachinas return from Walpi to kachina resting place.
39. Hemis Kachinas sing facing the kneeling Kachin'manas at Walpi.
40. A line of Niman Kachinas at Oraibi.
41. Hemis Kachinas gather in the plaza at Walpi.
42. Niman Kachina holds forth a bow and arrows.
43. Members of the Powamu society gather to cast their prayer meal upon the Niman Kachinas at Walpi.
44. The principals in the Niman ceremony cluster about the entrance to the Chief Kiva at Walpi.
45. The Kachina Chief leads ritual circuit of Eototo, Kachin'Mana and the Hemis Kachinas about the hatchway of the Chief Kiva.
46. Three Hopi men struggle outside of a house at Oraibi.
47. Town of Oraibi.
48. Snake men gather for their hunt around the Snake Kiva.
49. Snake men descend First Mesa to gather snakes.
50. A long line of boys and girls bearing cornstalks rush up the side of Walpi.
51. The winner of the Antelope race rushes into the north plaza at Walpi.
52. Snake youth carries the Snake banner across the plaza at Walpi.
53. Snake priests circle the plaza as each pick up a snake and begins to dance.
54. The Kaletaka stands on the sand shoulder near Sun Spring below Walpi.
55. Alosaktaka stands awaiting the formation of the procession that will make its way up the trail into Walpi.
56. Members of the flute society sit praying at the edge of Sun spring below First Mesa.
57. Women chase a man playing Ya-ha-ha.
58. A chorus of men sing in the plaza with Somaikoli, the Yaya priest, and the Yaya maiden.
59. Somaikoli being led by the Yaya priest.
60. Palhik'mana with the Palhik'taka dance in the plaza at Walpi.
61. Lakone women emerge from the Chivato Kiva at Walpi.
62. Two Lakone Manas enter the plaza at Walpi.
63. Men struggle in the Walpi plaza to retain a basket thrown out by the Lakone Manas.
64. Lakone society women perform a basket dance in the plaza at Walpi.
65. Members of all the societies cluster around the kiva hatch during the Wuwuchim ceremony.
66. Members of the Two-Horned priests' society perform their ritual at the Mong Kiva.
67. During the Wuwuchim rites members of the four Hopi societies perform a shuffling procession.
68. The Two-Horn society moves in a side-stepping line through Walpi.

THE HOPI PHOTOGRAPHS
KATE CORY: 1905-1912

1. AHÜL COMPLETES HIS FALSETTO CALL as he stands at the hatchway of the Mong Kiva in Walpi in the early morning. The kiva chief prepares to hand him prayer feathers.

"At sunrise...stooping down in front of the kiva hatch, Ahül drew a mark with meal upward on the inside of the front side of the hatchway, that is on the side opposite the ladder. He then turned to the sun and made six silent inclinations, then, standing erect, he bent his head backward and began a low rumbling growl and as he brought his head forward, raised his voice to a high falsetto."

HOPI JOURNAL
Alexander M. Stephen (1936)

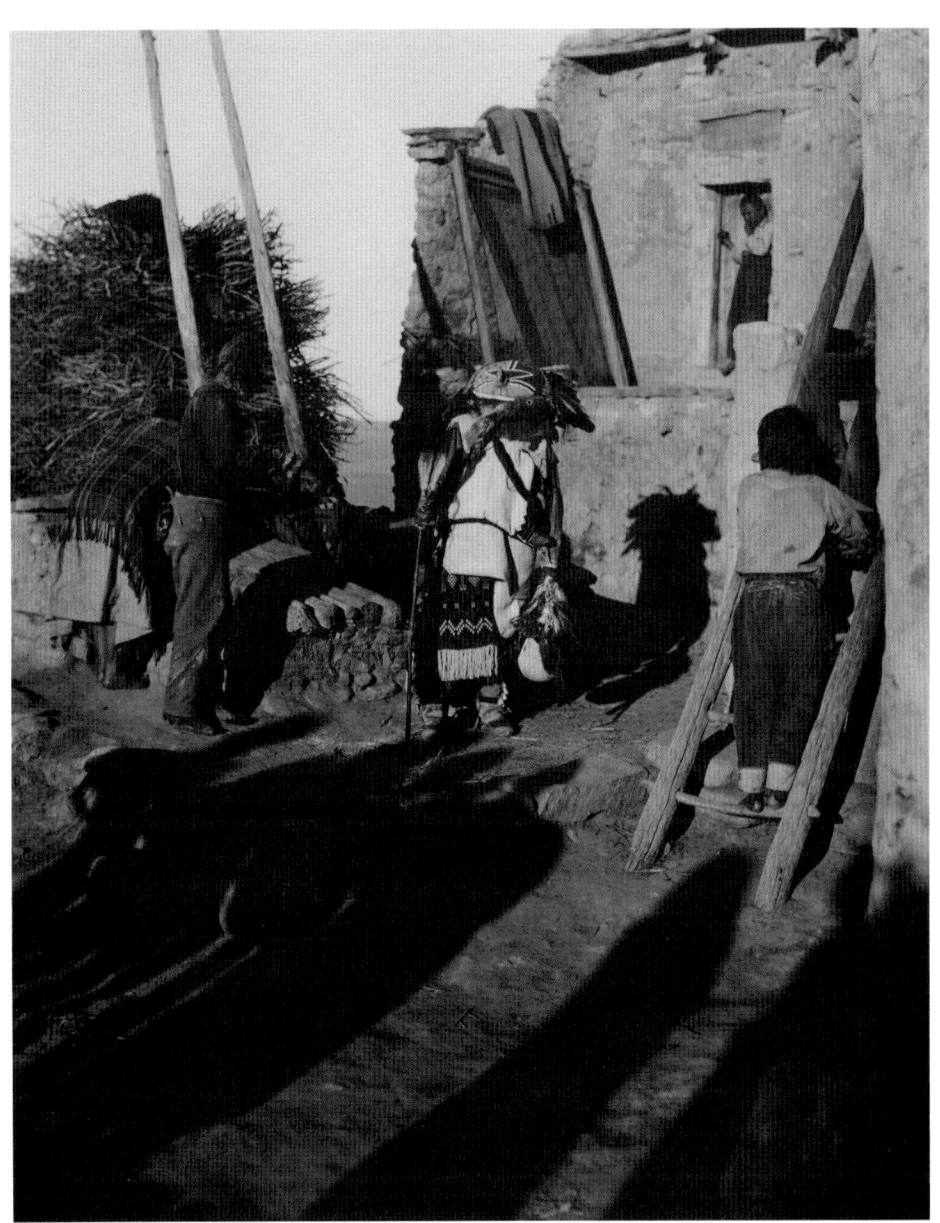

2. THE CHIEF FROM THE CHIVATO KIVA waits for Ahül to complete his falsetto call to the Sun before casting corn meal towards the kachina.

"Standing to the east of the hatch facing the opening, he bows down four times very slowly, saying 'ha-a-a-a-a' in a falsetto which lasts to the limit of his breath. After this he takes a handful of the finely ground white corn from his sack and, bending down, pastes it, on the lower side of the hatch. The kiva chief then comes out and sprinkles corn meal toward him four times, gives him four prayer-sticks, which the men in the kiva have made for him, and receives one of the nine bundles of corn (and beans) carried by Ahül."

NOTES ON HOPI CEREMONIES IN THEIR INITIATORY FORM IN 1927-28

Julian H. Steward (1931)

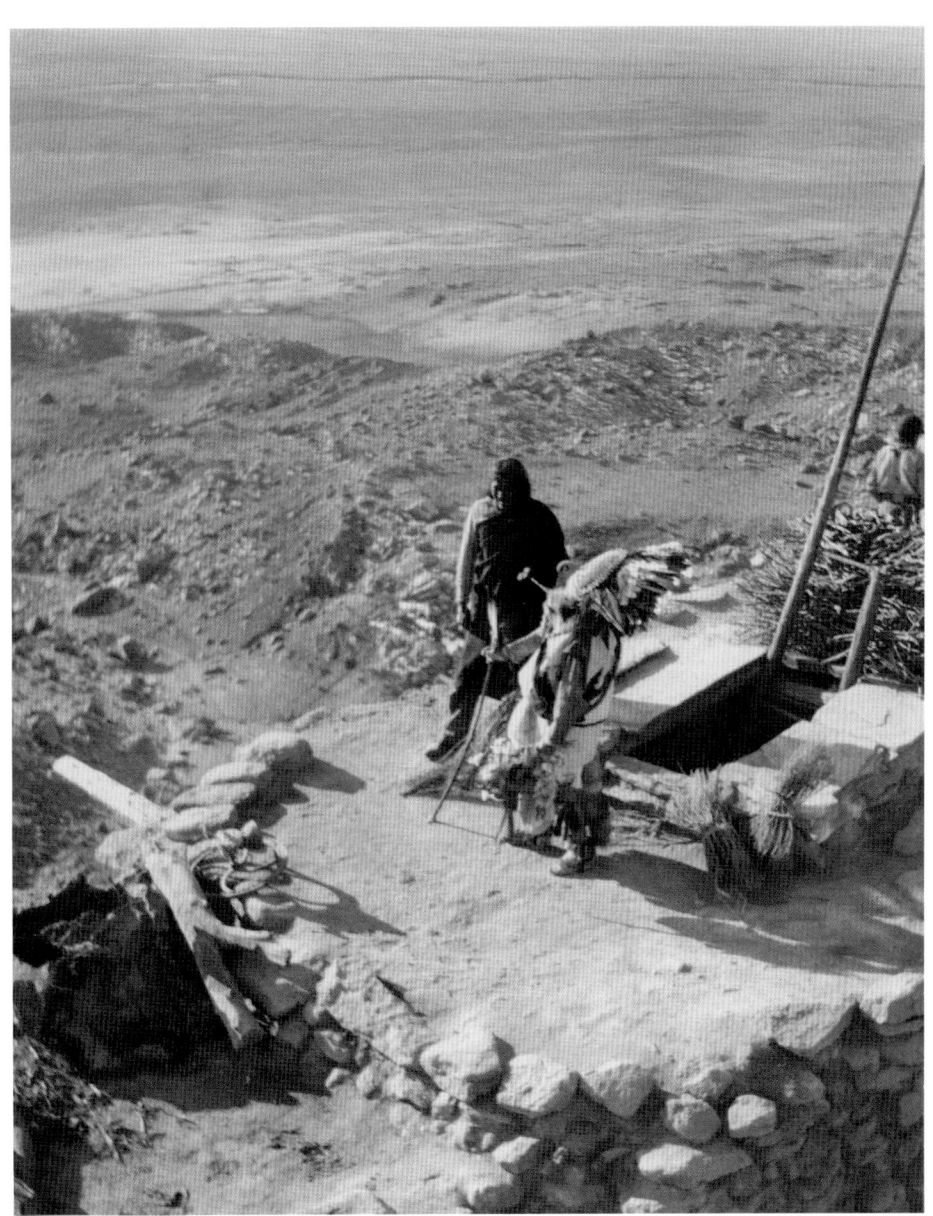

3. AHÜL PASSES THROUGH THE VILLAGE pausing at each clan or chief house to mark it. The marking of the houses strengthens them for the coming year, lending each supernatural support.

"At each house Ahül pastes cornmeal on the door, taking it in the palm of his hand and rubbing it from near the bottom of the door upward."

NOTES ON HOPI CEREMONIES IN THEIR INITIATORY FORM IN 1927-28

Julian H. Steward (1931)

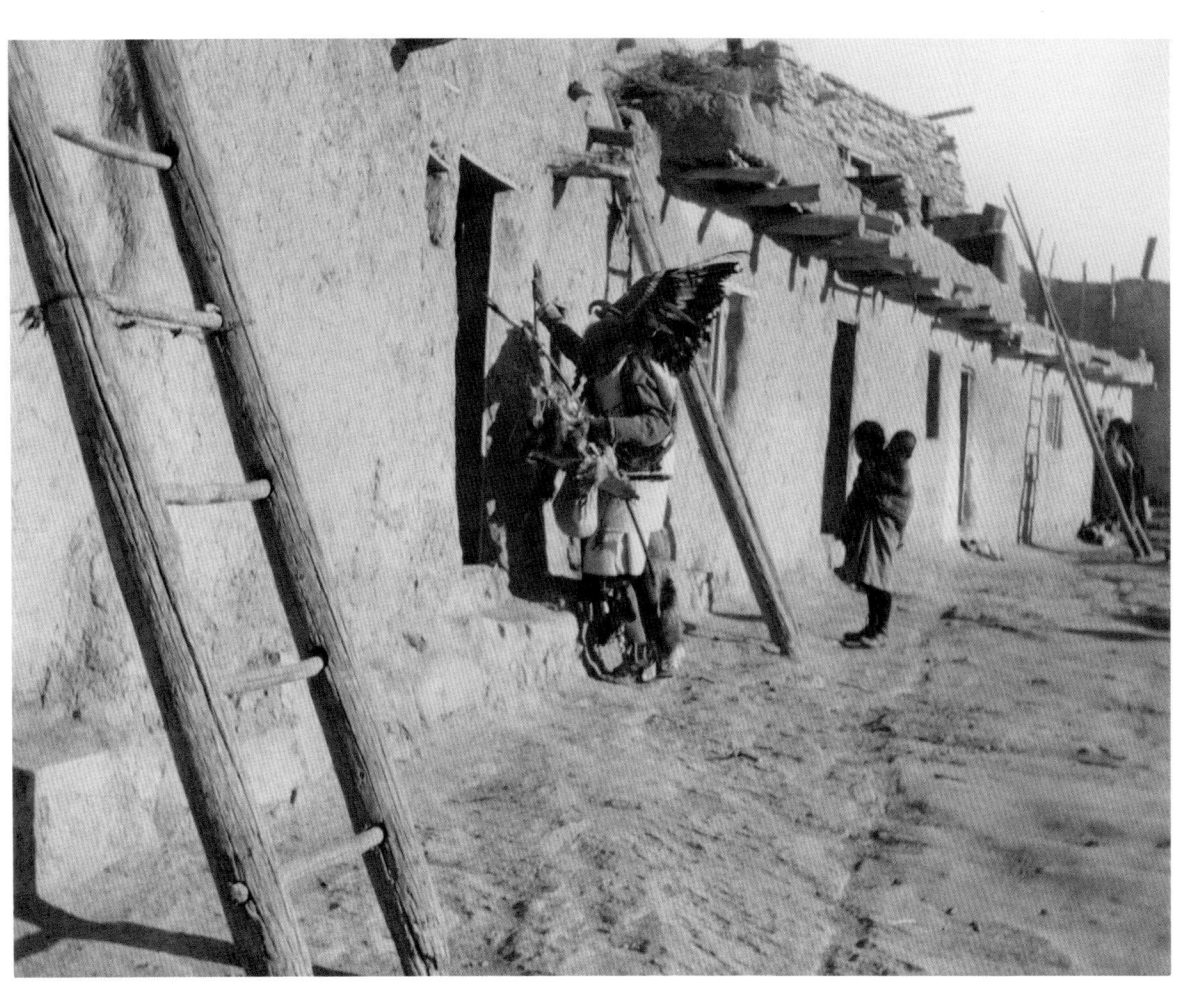

4. A LONG LINE OF KACHINAS in the Pachavu Ceremony move slowly up the southwest slope of Old Oraibi as they enter the village in late February.

"This long line slowly comes into sight from the south side of the village and makes its way to the place where the prayer stick is set in a hole in the plaza. Here each tray of beans is set down on each side of the hole for a moment."

HOPI KACHINAS
Edwin Earle and Edward Kennard (1938)

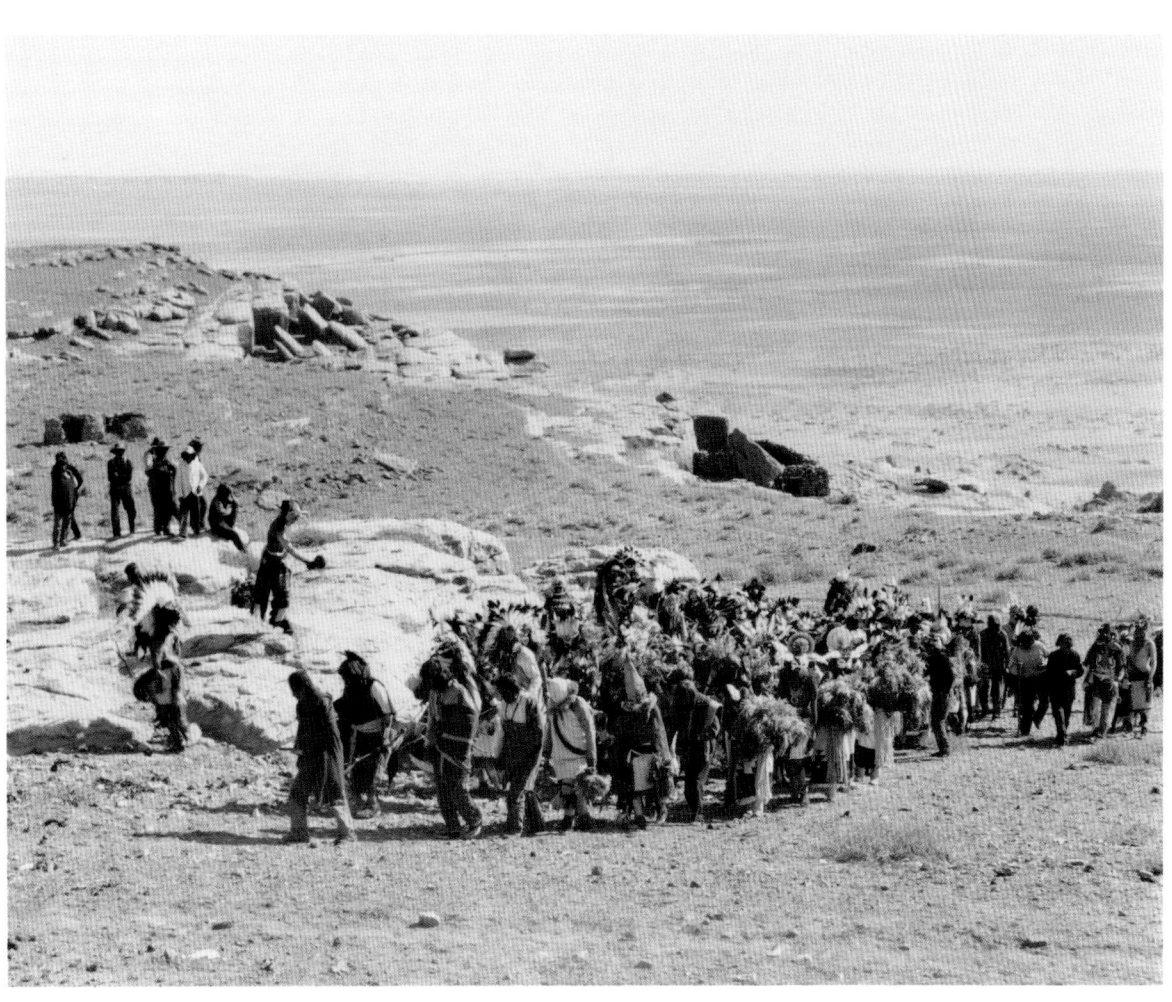

5. EOTOTO AND AHOLI, in the tall peaked mask, address their attention to the cloud symbol on the ground as the kachina chiefs watch.

"*Eototo goes first and draws a cornmeal symbol on the ground (⊕). This is supposed to represent the houses of the village, and Aholi puts his long staff at the junction of the middle vertical line with the horizontal and slowly revolves it towards him from the right to left while he issues a long, drawn-out cry.*"

OLD ORAIBI: A STUDY OF THE
HOPI INDIANS OF THIRD MESA

Micha Titiev (1944)

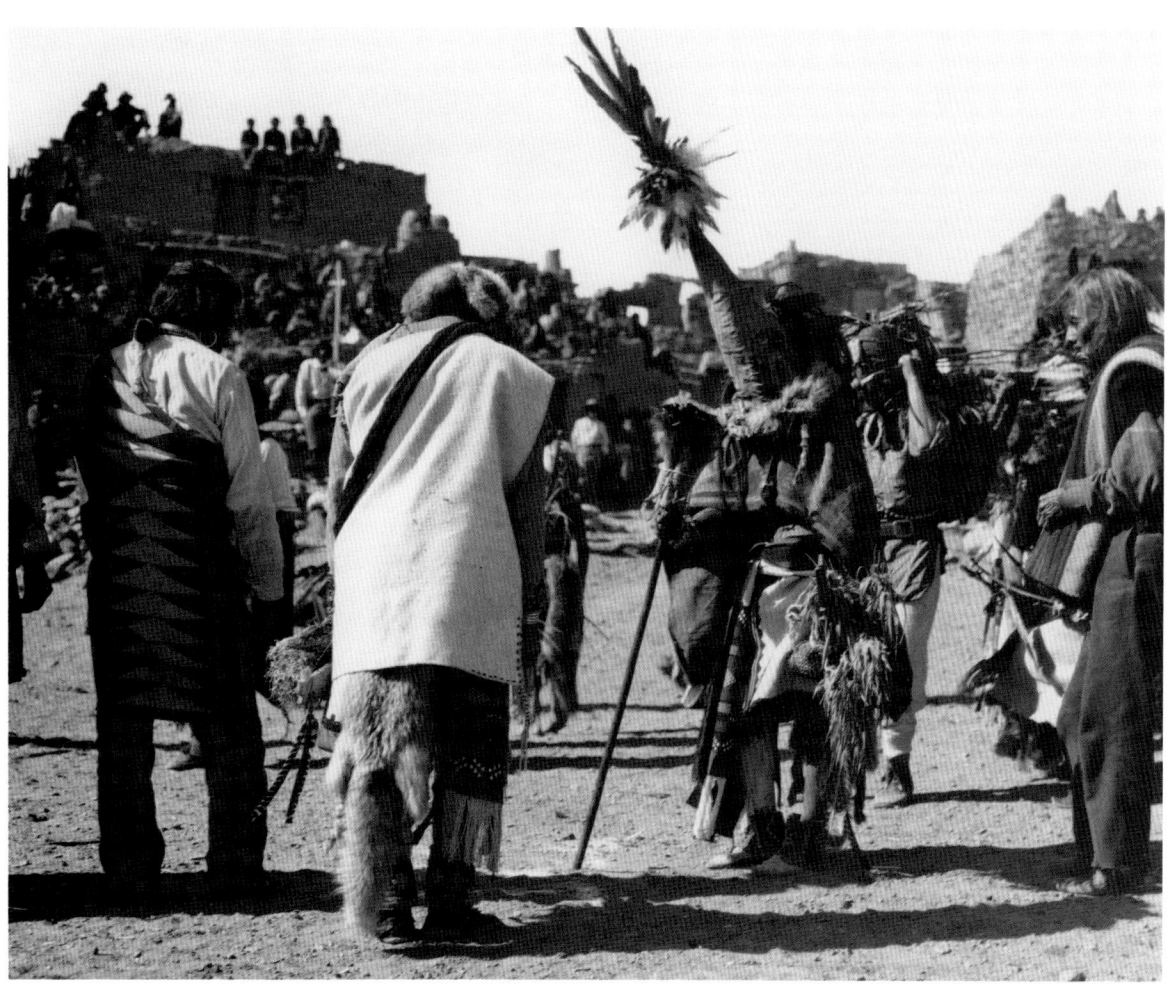

6. THE CROW MOTHER, Angwusnasomtaka or Tumas, prepares to enter a kiva as the kiva chief holds her yucca whips. Behind her stand the two whippers, the Hu' or Tungwup Kachinas.

"Suddenly, a great commotion is heard above...rattles and bells sound, the call of the dreaded Hu' Kachina comes down through the opening. There is tramping and beating on the roof of the kiva. Finally they enter, two Hu' Kachinas and Angwusnasomtaka. The latter is a figure of great dignity. In her hands she holds a number of whips of yucca blades tied together at the base."

HOPI KACHINAS
Earle and Kennard (1938)

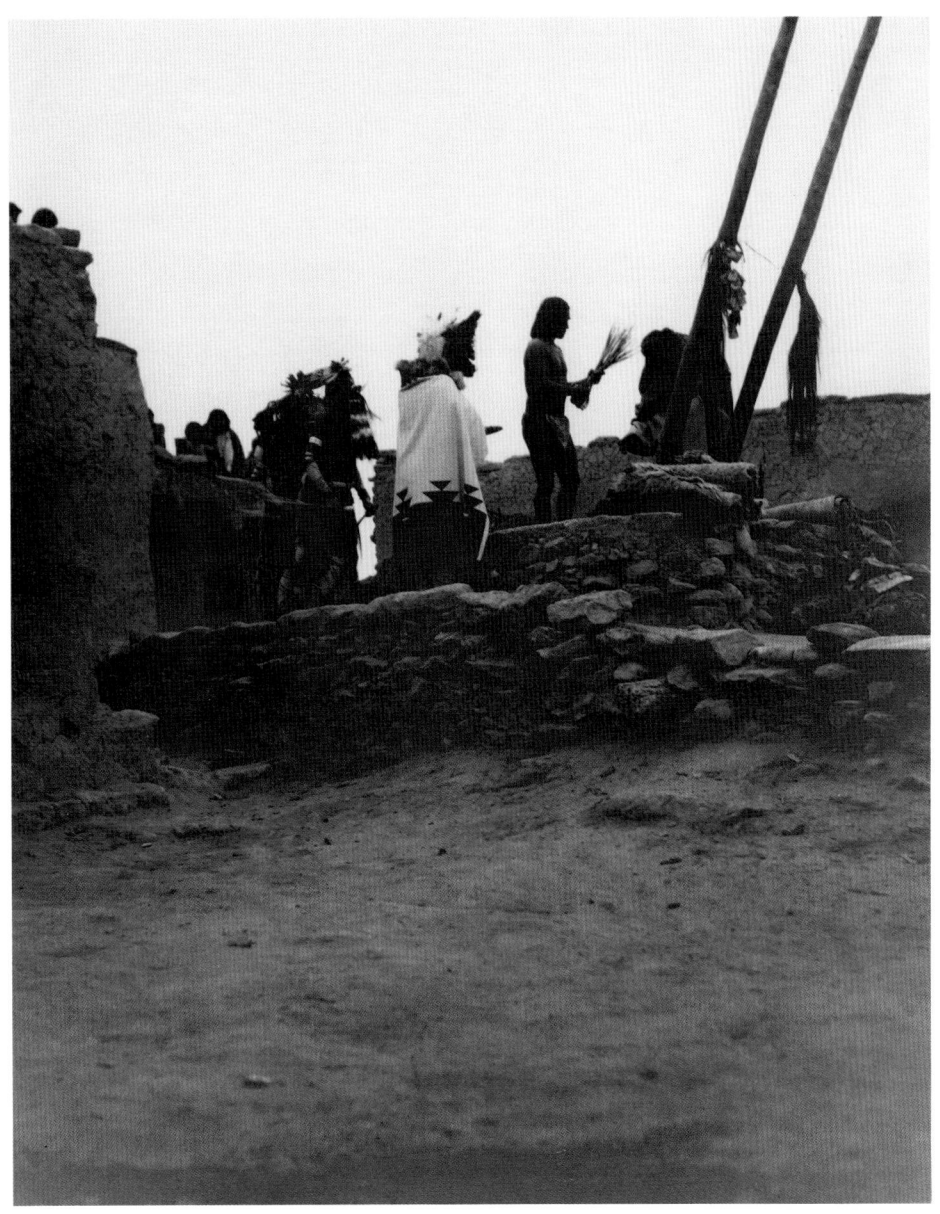

7. LED BY A HEHEYA KACHINA, a white, blue, and two black Nataskas stamp and growl before a house in Sichomovi during the Soyoko ceremony.

"*At 11:30 a.m. Soyok Mana, Hahai-i Wuqti and the Natackas made a visit to all the houses. They were followed by two Hehea katcinas with bags and pouches of food recently received, and after them followed three black and two white Natackas. These five went together and were constantly in motion, moving or beating time with their feet.*"

THE GROUP OF TUSAYAN CEREMONIALS CALLED KATCINAS

Jesse Walter Fewkes (1897)

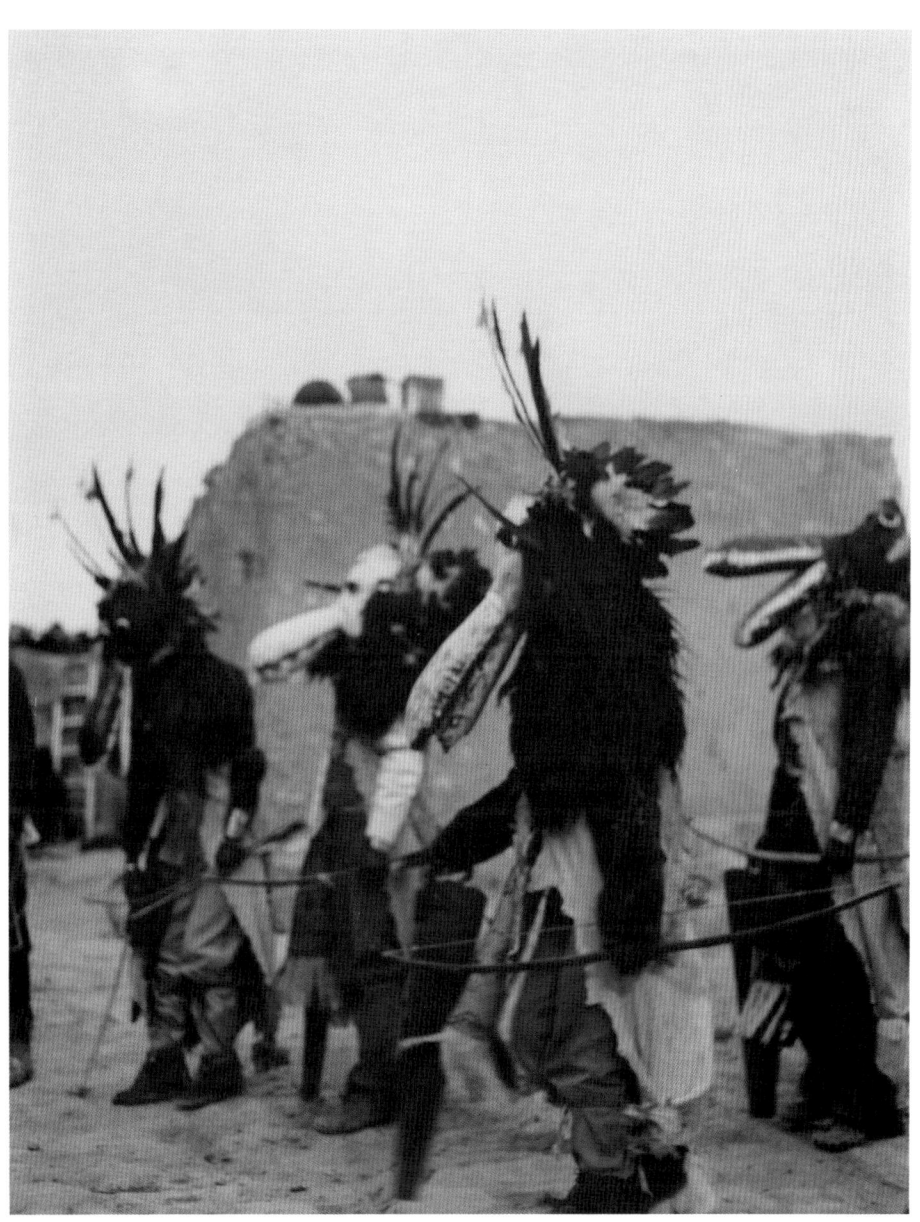

8. ONE OF THE HEHEYA RECEIVES a dish of corn flour from the occupant of a house as Hahai-i Wuhti looks on. Behind her stands the black Nataska stamping and growling.

"As the Soyoko went through the villages, they muttered and talked in falsetto voices. From house to house they went, and at each door Hahai-i woman addressed the child: 'We have come for the rabbit which we told you to kill for us.' "

NOTES ON HOPI CEREMONIES IN
THEIR INITIATORY FORM 1927-28

Julian Steward (1931)

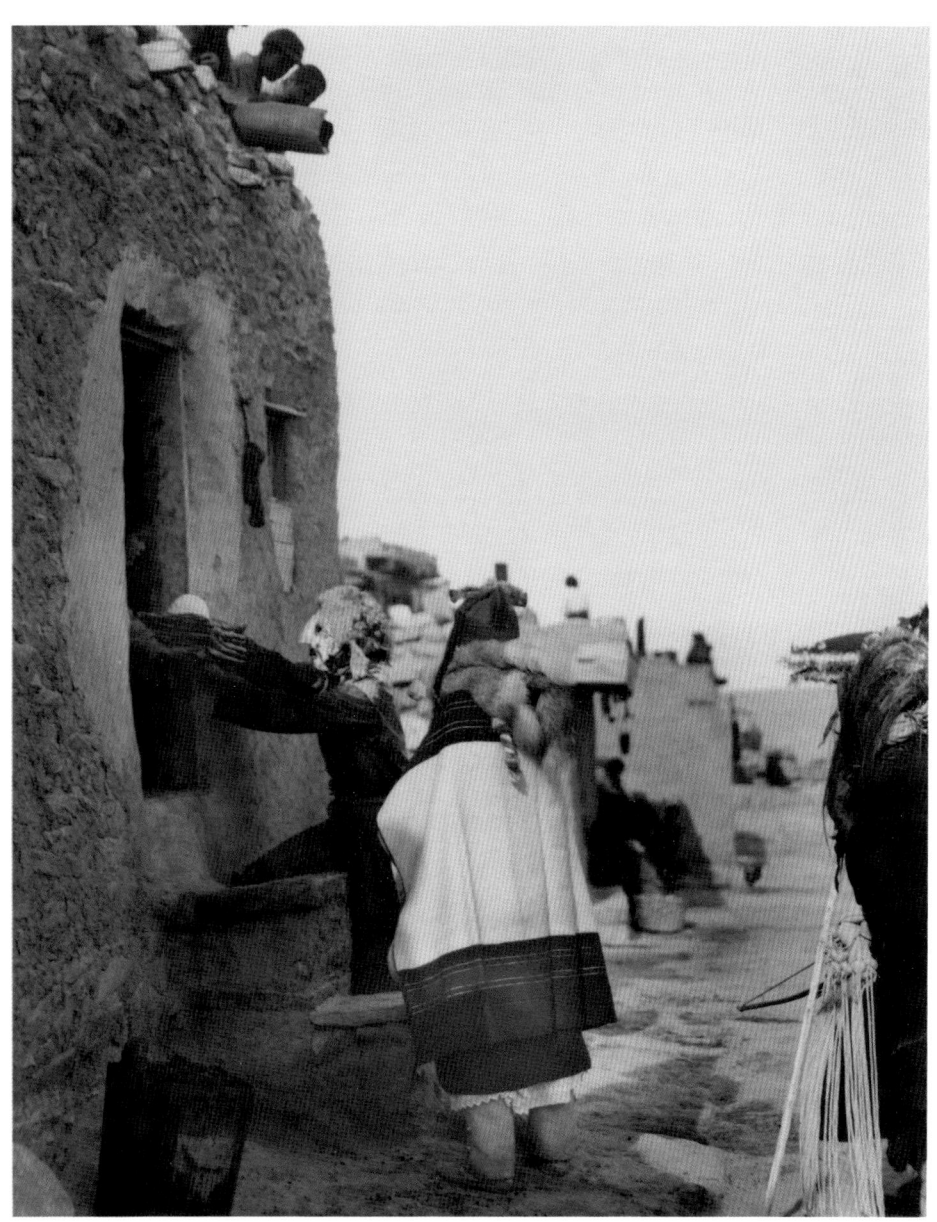

9. A YOUNG HOPI girl ceremonially dressed in full length white boots, the red and white maiden shawl, and wearing butterfly whorls contemplates the valley below her. The elaborate hairdress of the unwed Hopi girls caught the attention of every visitor to these people. It represents the flower of the squash, although it is often called butterfly wings as well. The great circular whorls do indeed resemble butterfly wings when seen from the side.

"The dressing of the hair in these peculiar whorls (or squash blossoms) requires hours of the mother's time. It is the symbol of womanhood."

INDIANS OF THE ENCHANTED DESERT
Leo Crane (1925)

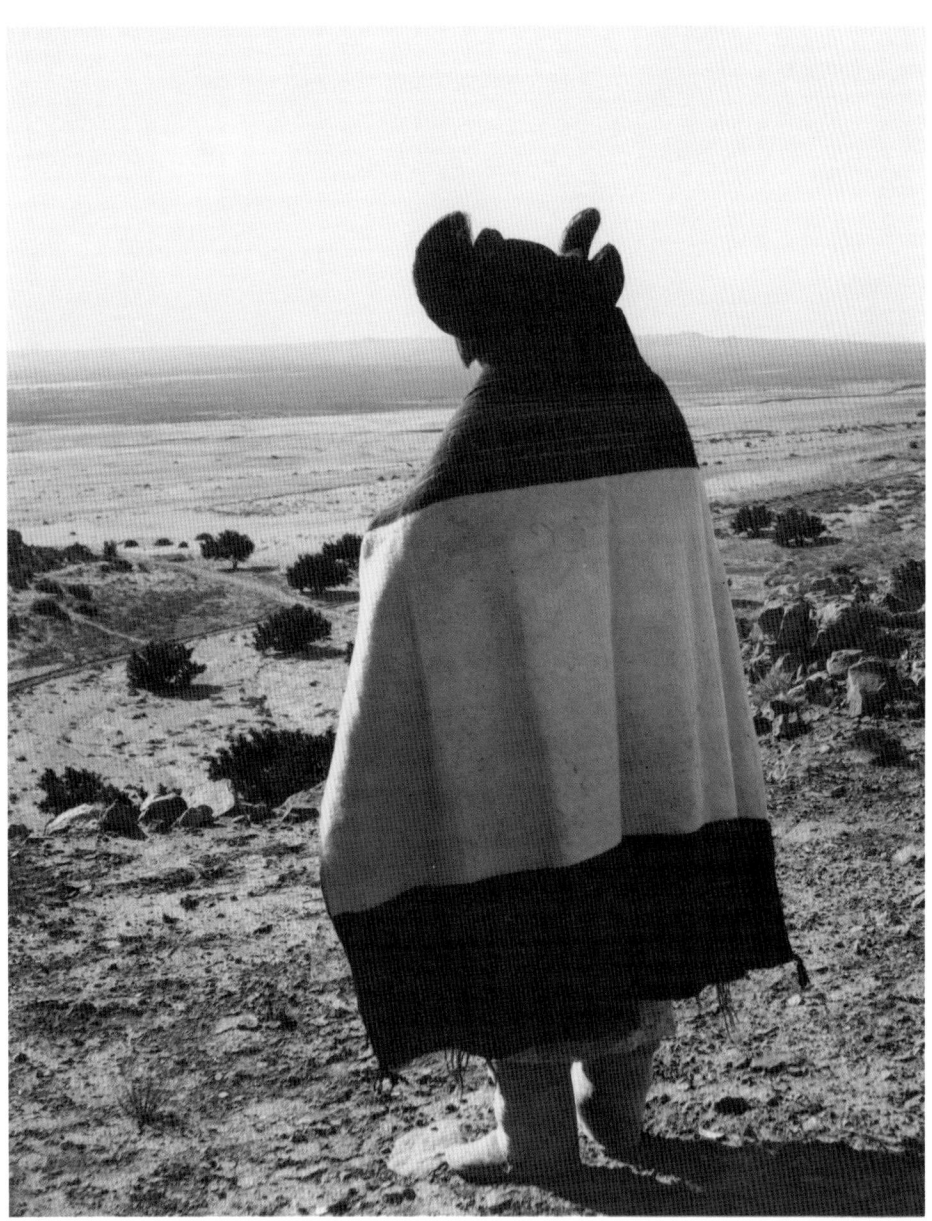

10. A YOUNG HOPI GIRL wearing the traditional butterfly hair whorls and maiden shawl.

"Only one old man had a definition of a pretty girl, which was in terms of ancient dress: she wears her hair in butterfly whorls, whitens her face with corn meal, wears a woolen dress (manta), and goes bare armed, bare legged, and bare foot…"

HOPI OF SECOND MESA
Ernest and Pearl Beaglehole (1935)

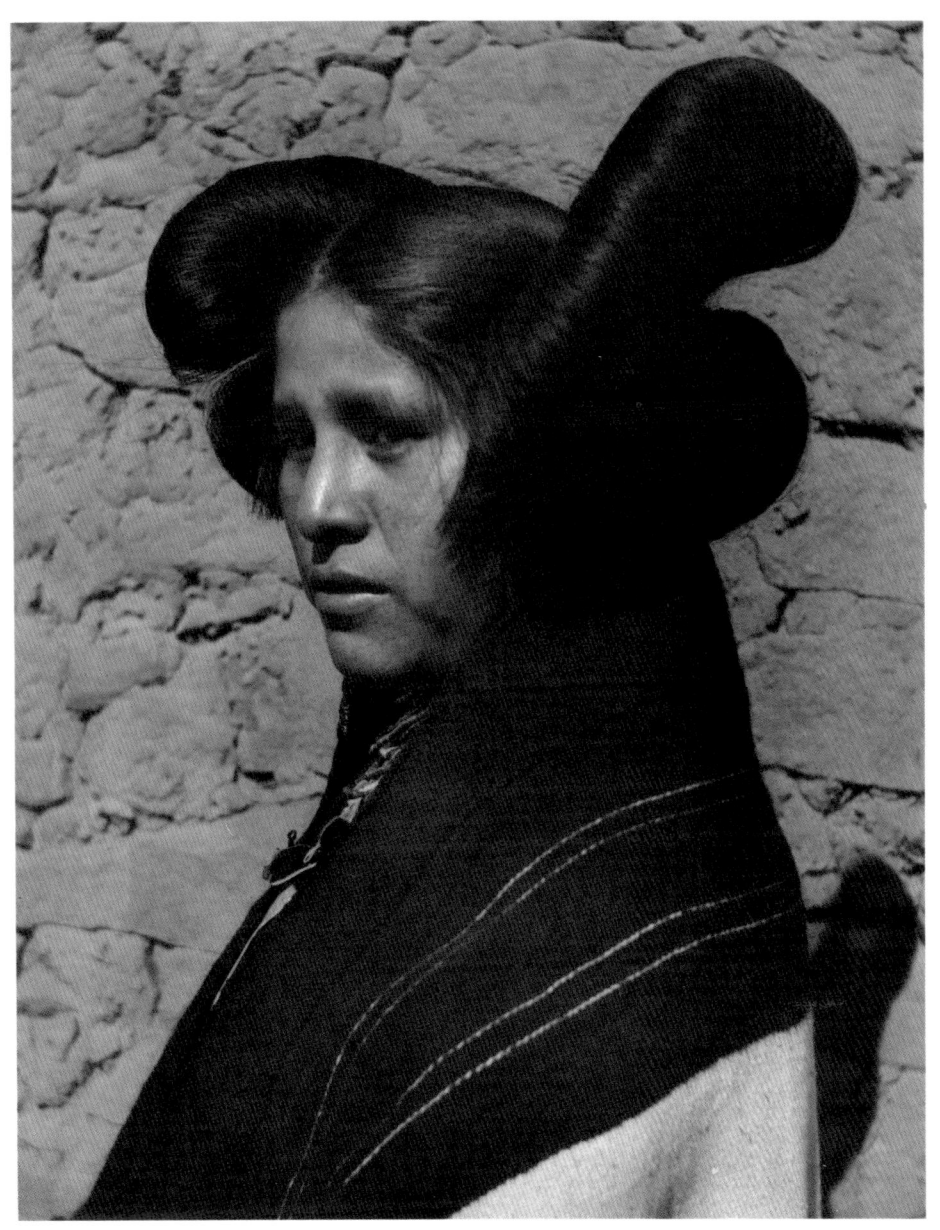

11. From the kiskya or passageway through the center of Walpi, a Hopi girl looks across the wide valley of Polacca Wash. Dressed in the fabrics of the white man's school she goes barefoot in the manner of her own people.

"The younger women, who have had schooling, wear the gingham and calico dresses they have learned to make and launder, and the field matrons assist them in renewing these garments."

Indians of the Enchanted Desert
Leo Crane (1925)

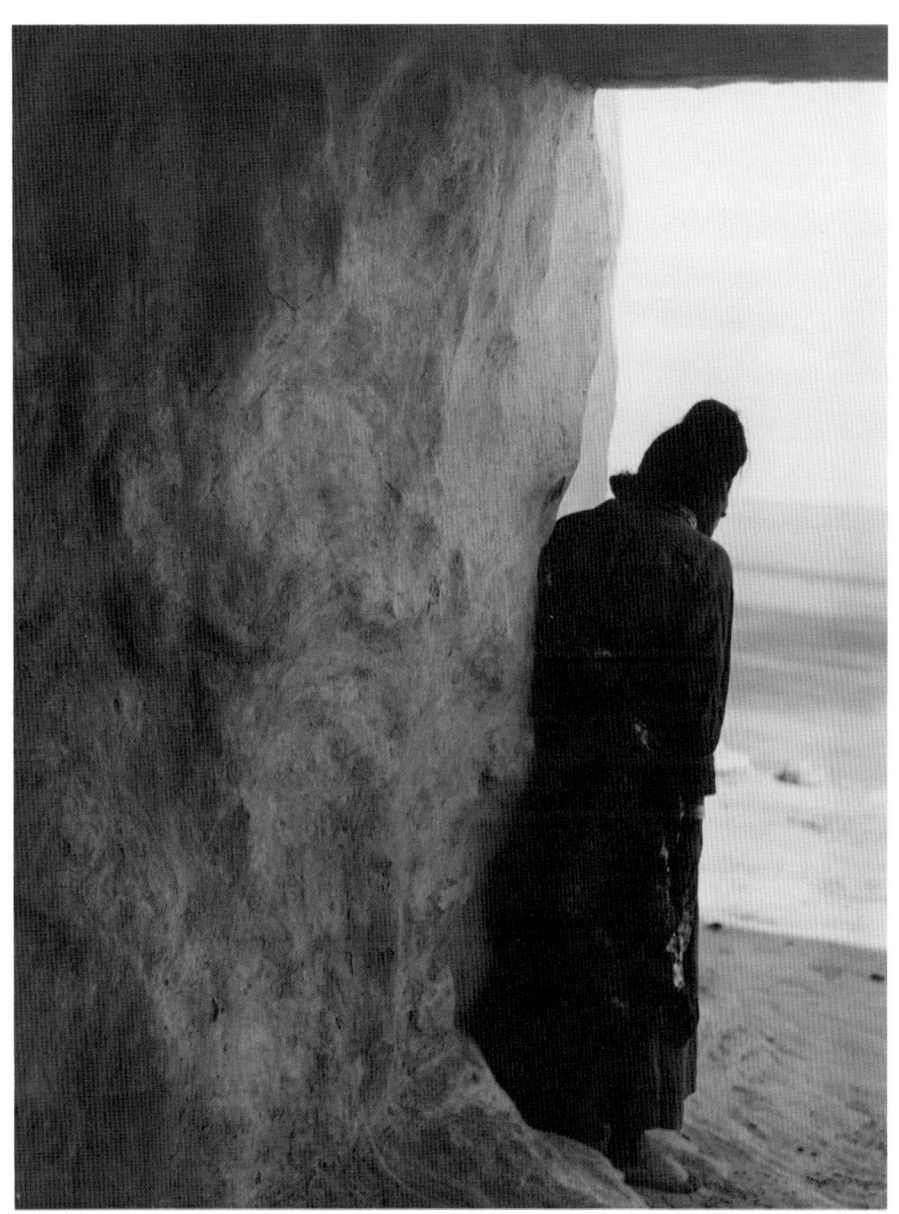

12. A Hopi man carries a dead infant to the cemetery.

"I took the dead baby and buried him in the tomb with his brothers and sisters, but, oh, how I hated to do it. In bitterness and sorrow I said, 'Now this is the last child that I shall have, for they all die.'"

SUN CHIEF, AUTOBIOGRAPHY OF A HOPI INDIAN

Don Talayesva from Leo Simmons (1942)

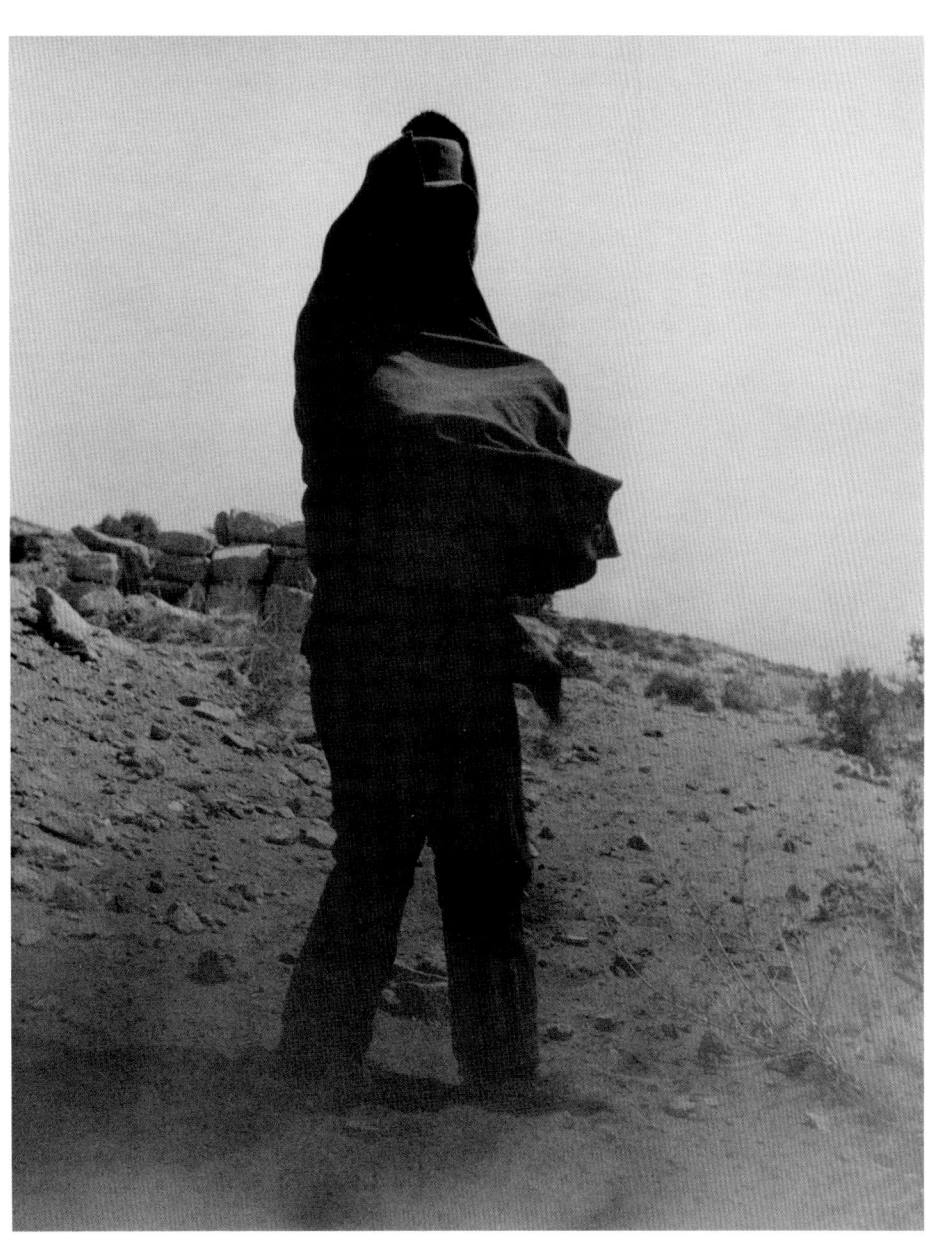

13. A LINE OF ANAK'CHINA, the bringers of gentle rain, enter the plaza at Sichomovi.

"They are dancing. Barbarically beautiful, brilliantly colored. Gently waving their twigs of spruce, shaking their gourd rattles. Singing like the soughing of the wind through the pines. Stamping rythmically as the beat of the drum, insistently as the pulse of the earth."

MASKED GODS
Frank Waters (1950)

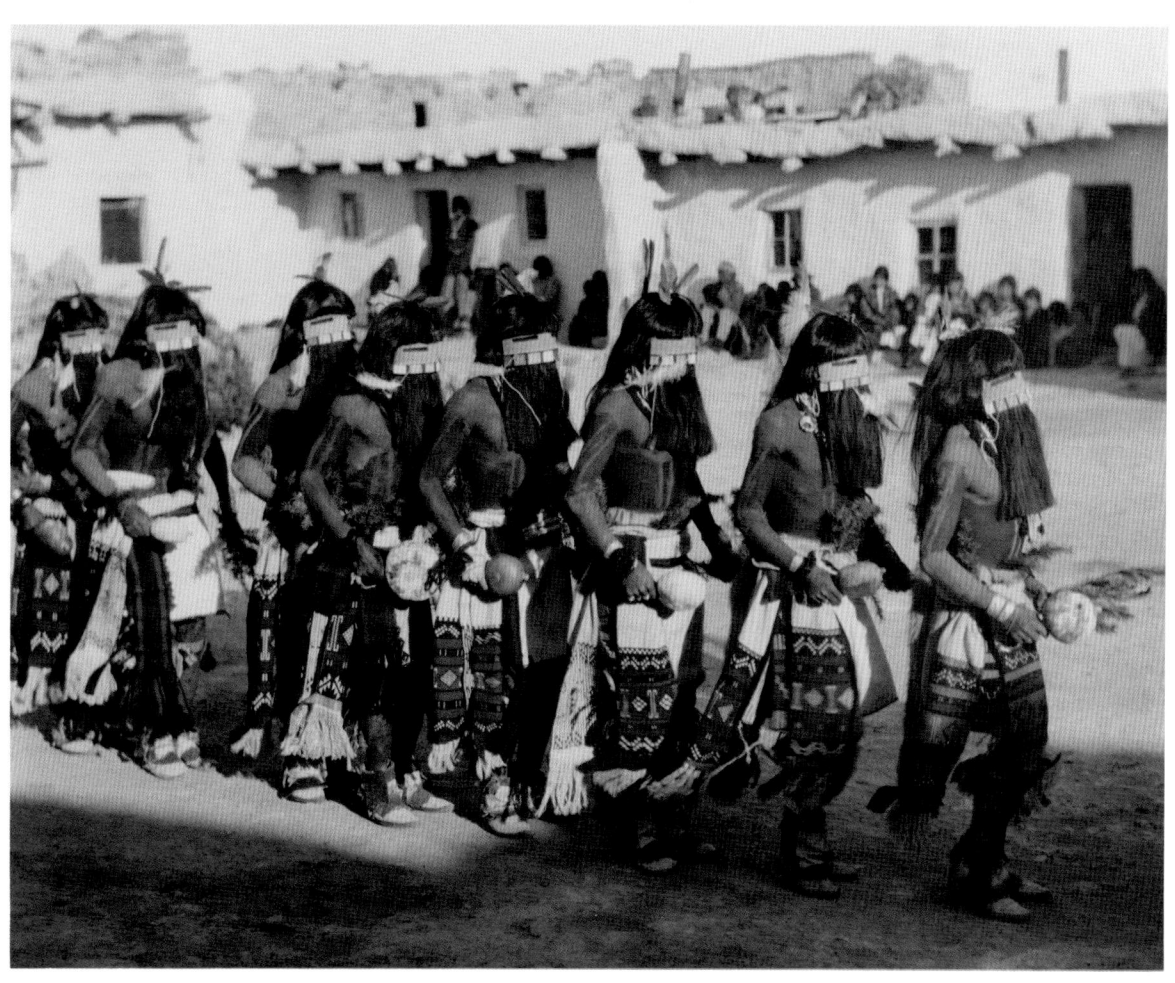

14. A GROUP OF HOPI MOCK their Navajo neighbors with the antics of the Tasavu clowns in the plaza at Shipaulovi.

"During the absence of the dancers from the plaza, special groups of clowns, wearing grotesque masks and clothing in keeping with the character impersonated, enter the plaza. Sometimes they are Navajos, sometimes they stage a mock Hopi wedding, sometimes they ridicule government officials and school teachers."

HOPI KACHINAS
Edwin Earle and Edward Kennard (1938)

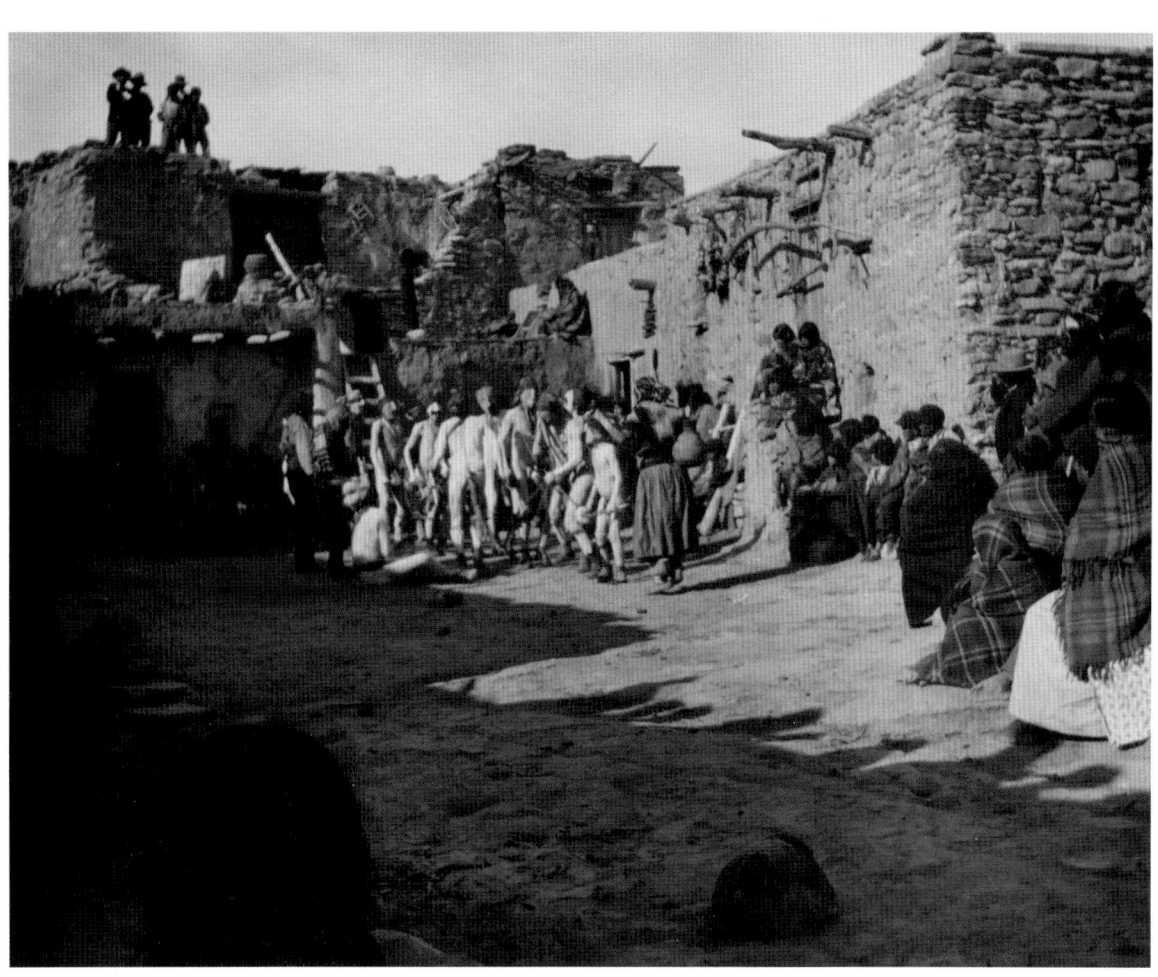

15. A SINGLE MA-ALO KACHINA dances on the rooftops of Walpi. Reputed to be a Zuni-derived kachina it was very popular around the turn of the century. It brings gentle rain and good crops.

"The different Ma-lo-ka-tci-nas carried in the hand a staff or na-tuk-pi...some were straight and some had crooks at the end. The straight kind were painted black and green, and at the end had tied to them two of the tail feathers of the eagle..."

A FEW SUMMER CEREMONIALS
AT THE TUSAYAN PUEBLOS

Jesse Walter Fewkes (1892)

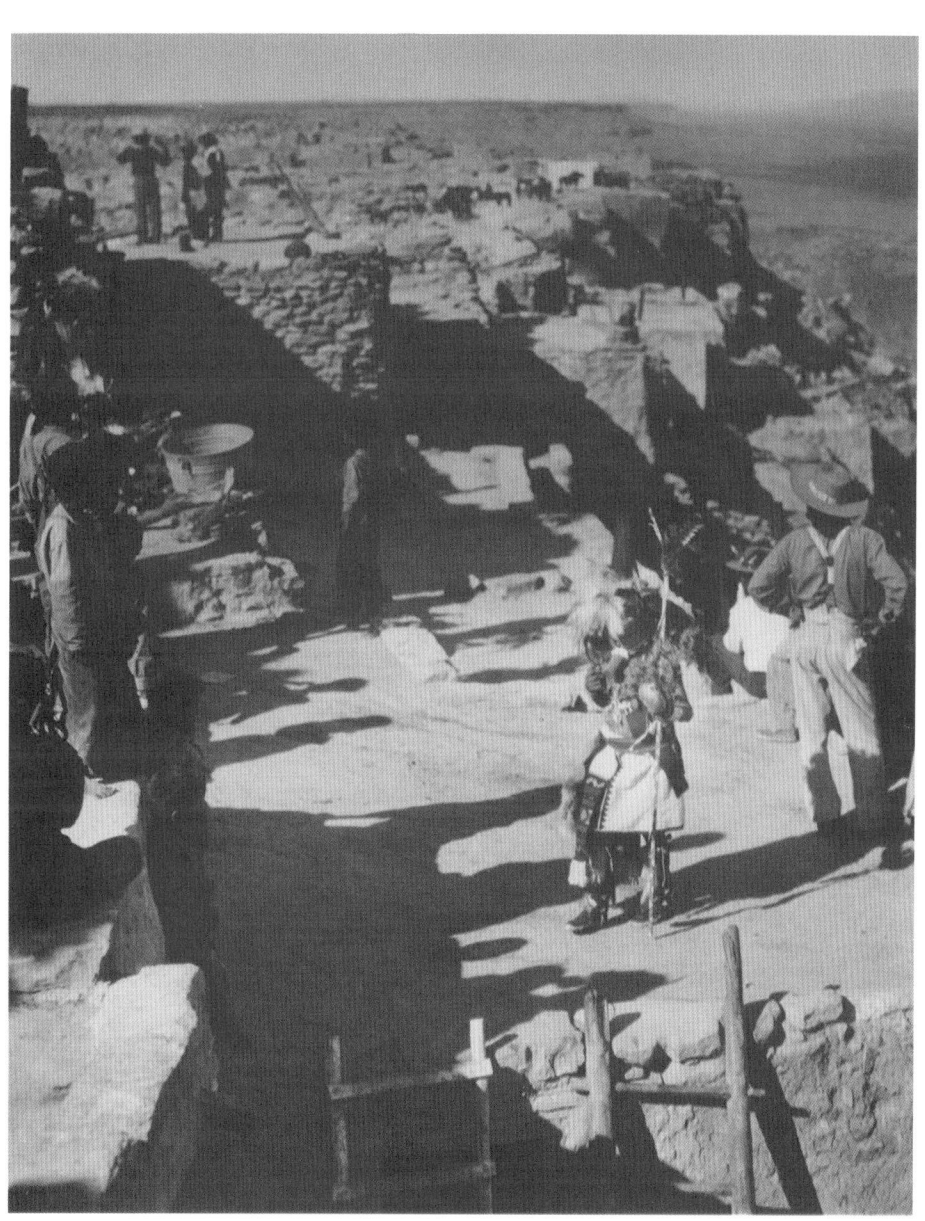

16. A LINE OF CHAKWAINA KACHINAS moves into position as their Koyemsi drummer prepares to start the singing. The kachina father stands beside the drummer. The Chakwaina Kachinas were brought to Hopi from Zuni.

"A bundle is beaten for certain Zuni kachina, the home Chakwena and the home Mixed dance. The bundle consists of different kinds of clothing or cloth and of jewelry wrapped very tight in a buckskin or today in a canvas wagon cover. Because of the valuable clothing and beads, people will come running to hear this bundle drum; at least this is what the Kachina chief says to all the things when he makes a bundle of them."

ZUNI KACHINAS
FORTY-SEVENTH ANNUAL REPORT OF THE BUREAU OF AMERICAN ETHNOLOGY. WASHINGTON.

Ruth Bunzel (1929-30)

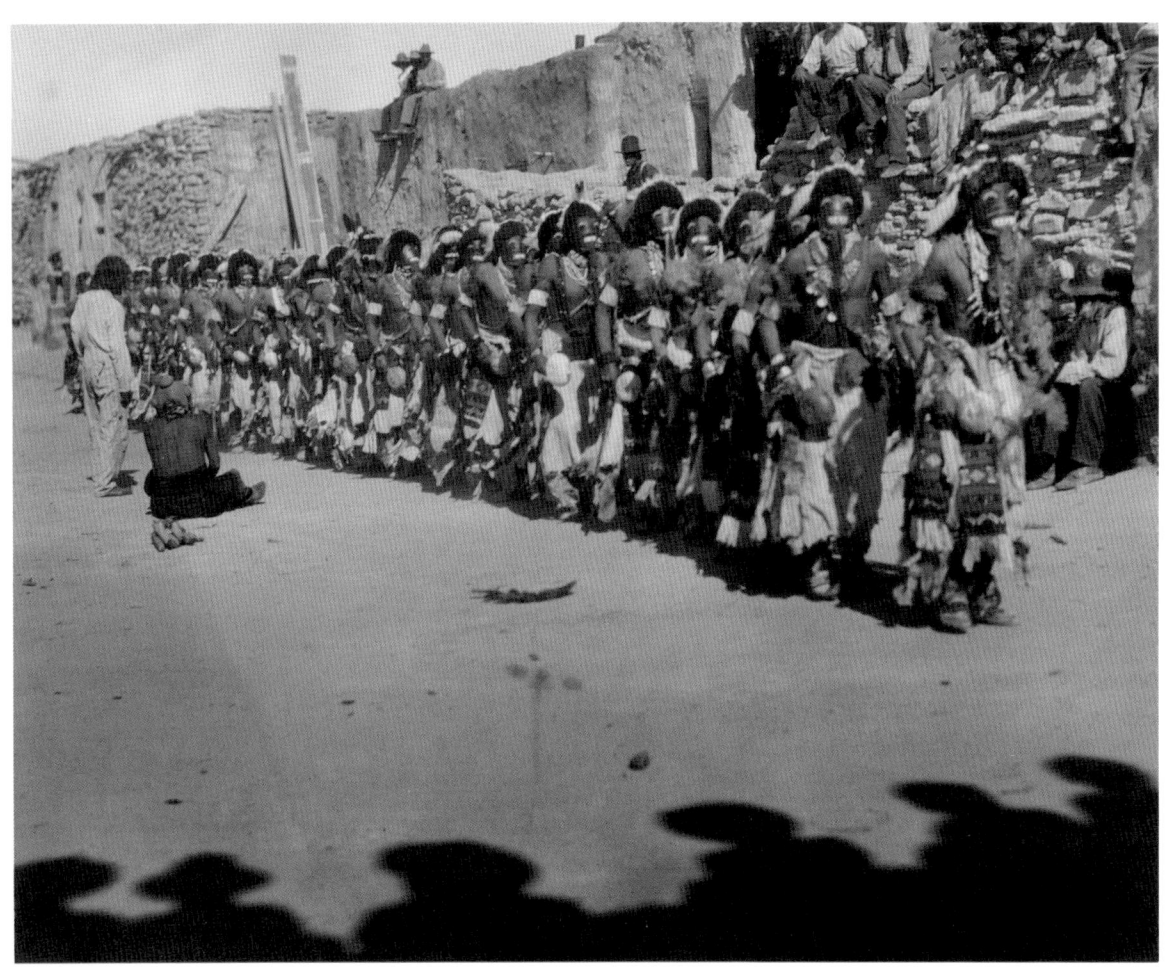

17. THE KACHINA DANCERS REST below the cliffs at Walpi out of sight of the children of the village. Removing their masks they eat an abundant meal. The women in the background have brought the food.

"Lots of people came from different towns. They had a big feast so everybody was very happy. The kachinas have a big dinner, too. The man who had this dance killed a steer and sheep, to give the kachinas dinner."

PUEBLO INDIAN JOURNAL 1920-21,
INTRODUCTION AND NOTES

Crow-Wing from Elsie Clews Parsons (1925)

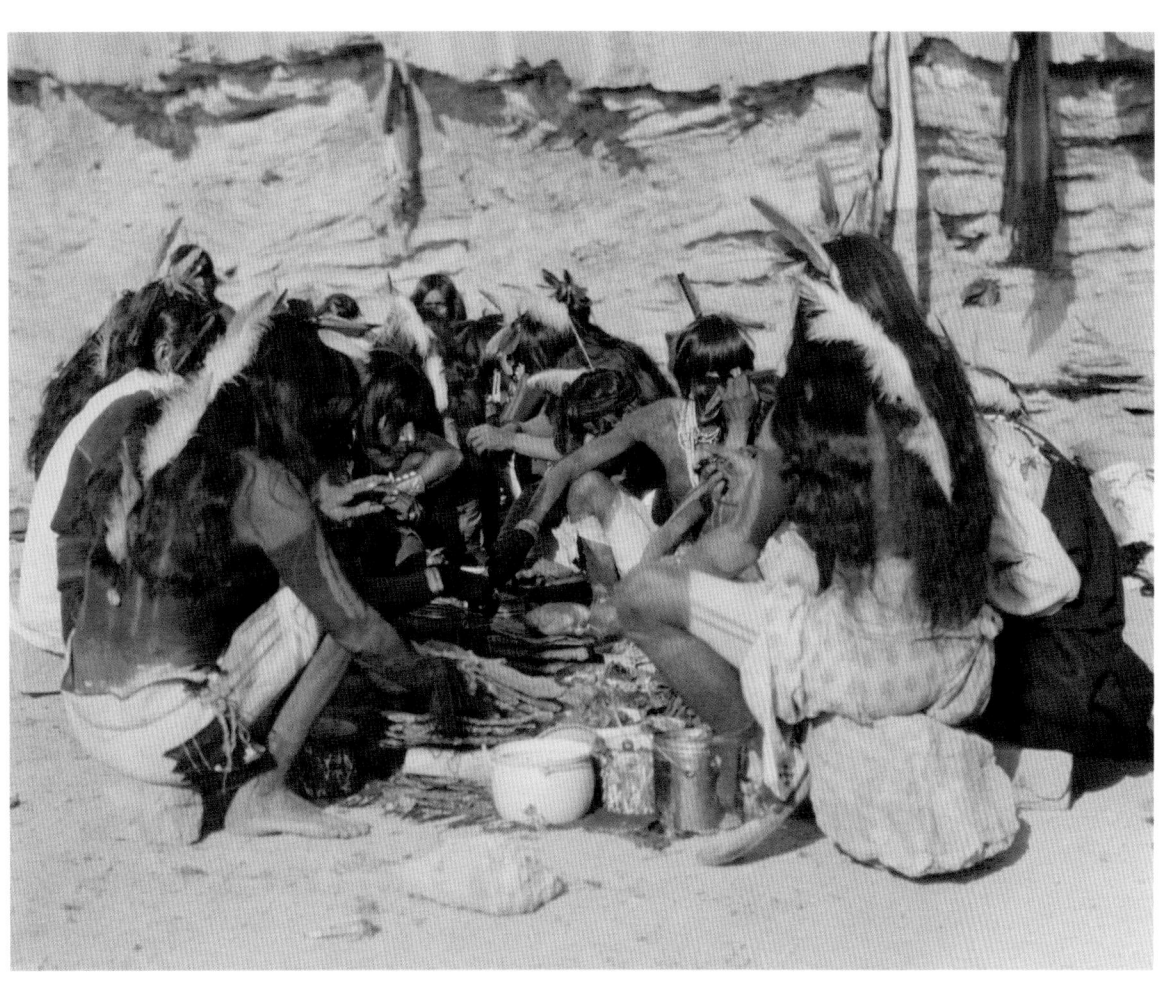

18. GAILY CLAD MEMBERS of a Mixed Kachina dance pause to rest at Kowawaima on First Mesa as the elders sit praying and smoking.

"The songs are repeated, and the dancers move to the north side facing west. After the songs are repeated in this position, the dancers leave the kisonvi and go to a secluded section of the mesa where they unmask, smoke, eat, and rest for a while. Following a brief rehearsal of the next song-set, they mask and return to the village for another round of dancing."

THE KACHINA AND THE WHITE MAN
Frederick J. Dockstader (1954)

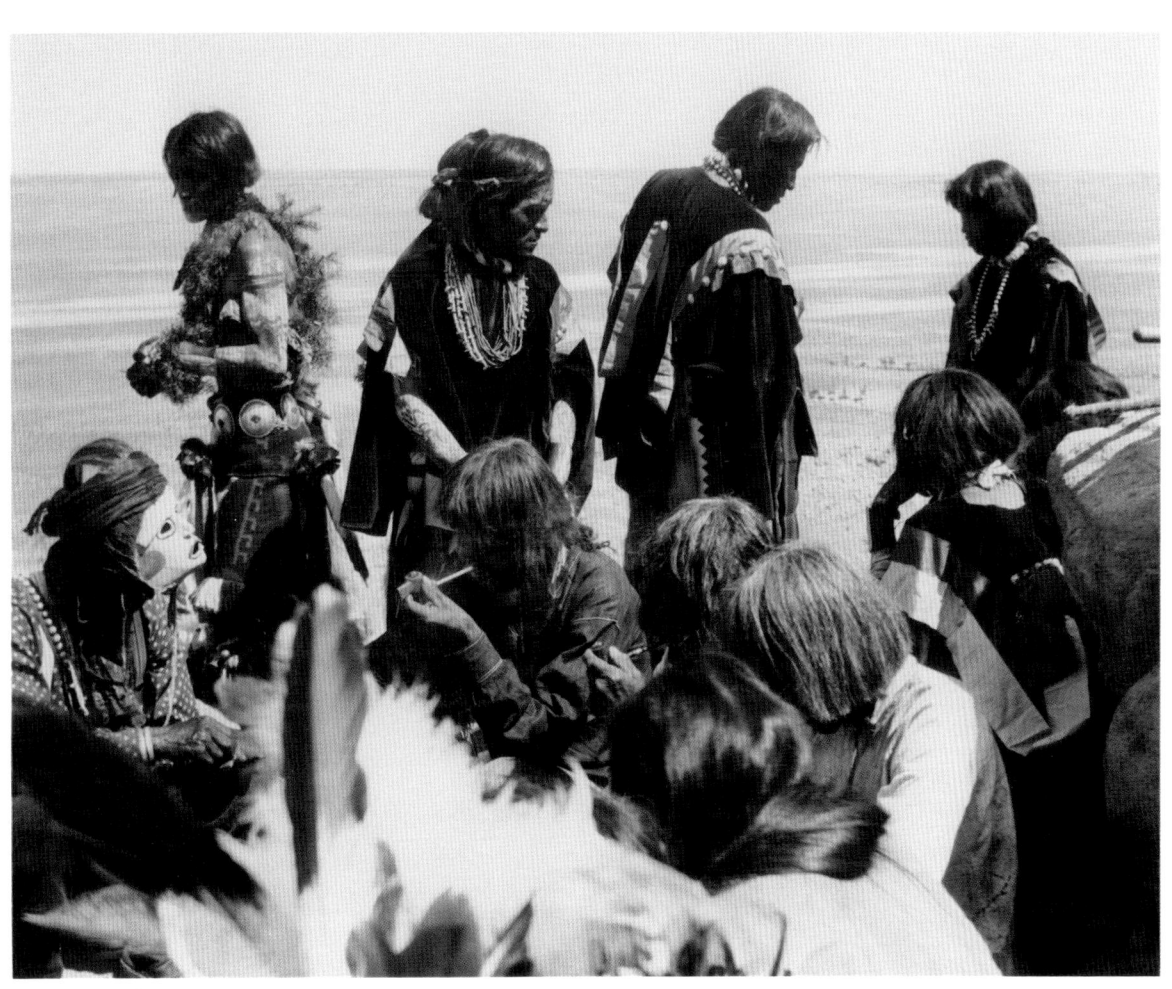

19. A PRECISE LINE OF NAVAN, Velvet Shirt, Kachinas move across the plaza at Walpi as they make their ceremonial circuit, dancing on all four "sides" of the cleared area.

"Most beloved and frequent use of these visitants are the kachinas who come from the San Francisco Peaks, the home of the clouds.... They arrive in March when the early beans are planted, and stay until August when the rainy season begins and when all the Hopi gather to bid them farewell. For the intervening months they are hovering near the towns and on many an afternoon the sound of their male singing floats from the Plazas. In these days when Hopi men have wage work, kachinas seem to come on Saturday afternoons. You may see in the sunlight a line of kilted figures prancing with military precision to the rhythm of their shaking rattles."

FIRST PENTHOUSE DWELLERS OF AMERICA
Ruth Underhill (1938)

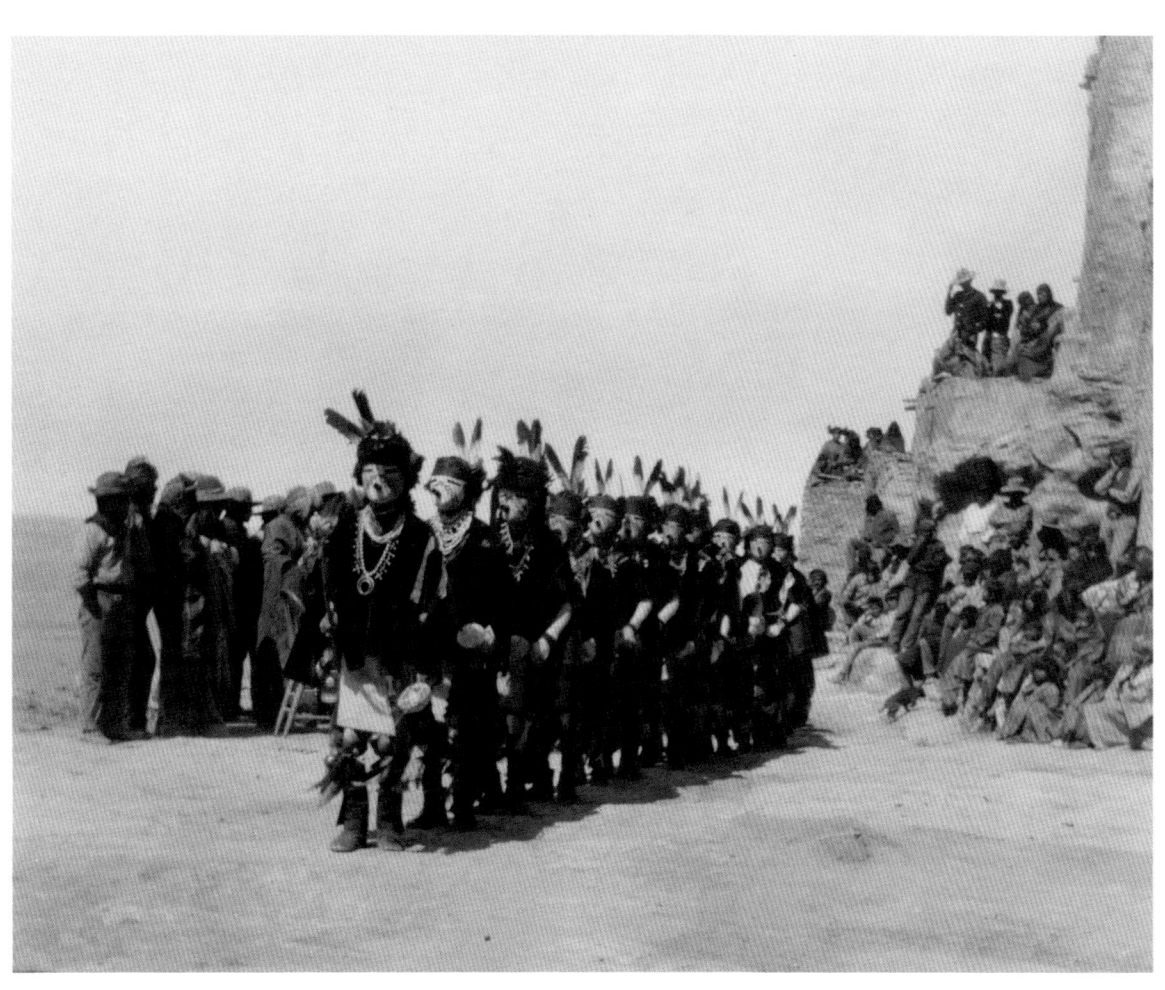

20. TWO COUPLES PERFORM the Buffalo dance in the plaza of Walpi on First Mesa.

"The Buffalo youth pranced about the Buffalo maid, now and then running the length of the plaza and pretending to spear the earth with his notched or zigzag stick. This action possibly symbolized the fertilization of the earth; indeed, one is tempted to suppose that it was a signature prayer to make the earth yield buffalos."

MINOR HOPI FESTIVALS
Jesse Walter Fewkes (1902)

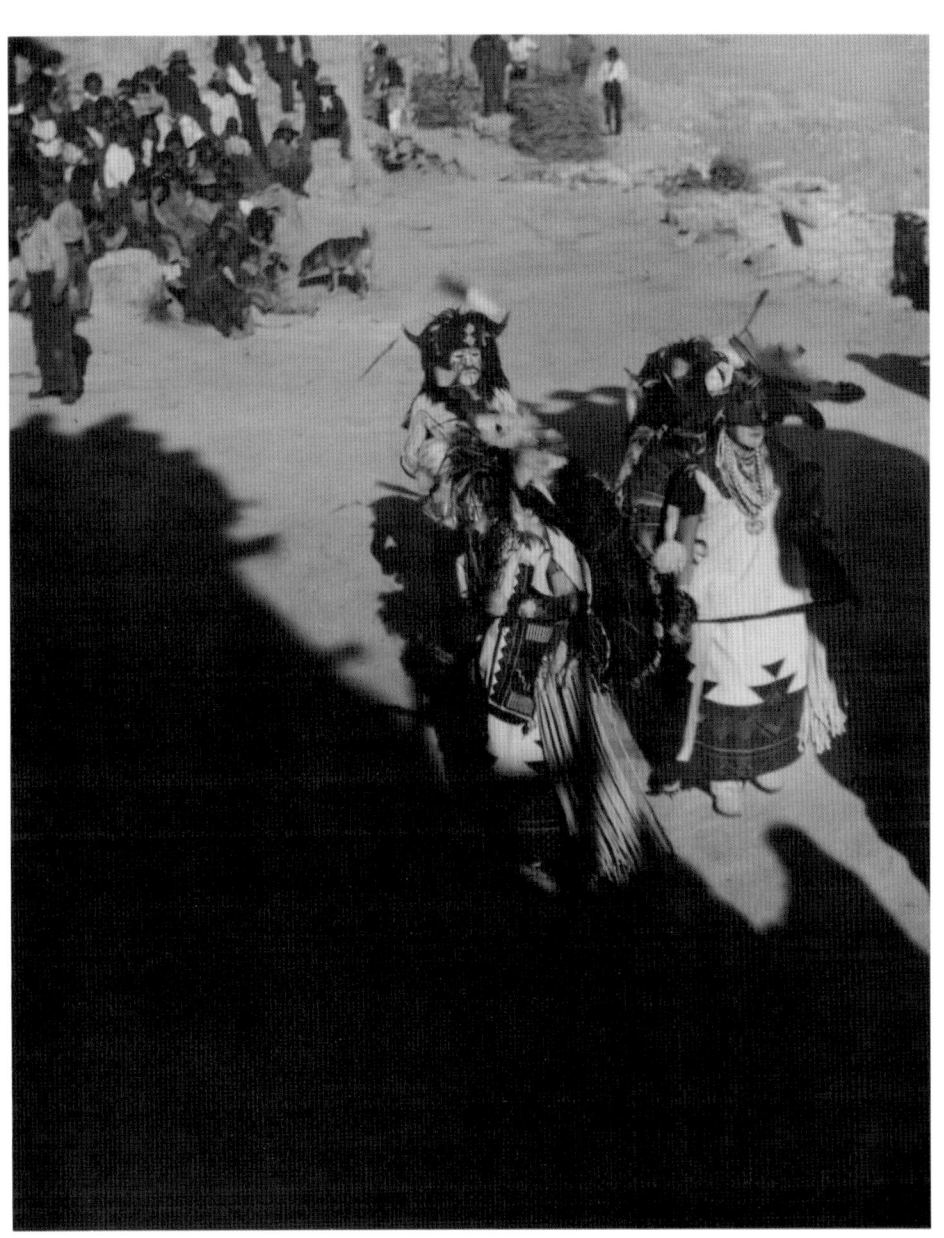

21. SUPELA OF WALPI, Patki Clan, Chief in the Winter Solstice and many other ceremonies.

"Supela assumed a part in everything. Great must be Supela's ability, since he is capable of counseling the numerous societies on any doubtful points in their rites and ceremonies. In fact, it seems that no observance in Walpi can get along without his aid, and even farther towns often call upon him to assist them in delicate points involved in the conduct of their religious celebrations.... Nervous of movement, cordial but occupied with pressing business, going somewhere, has scarcely time to more than ask a few curious questions, he seems to have the burden of Atlas on his shoulders."

THE HOPI INDIANS
Walter Hough (1915)

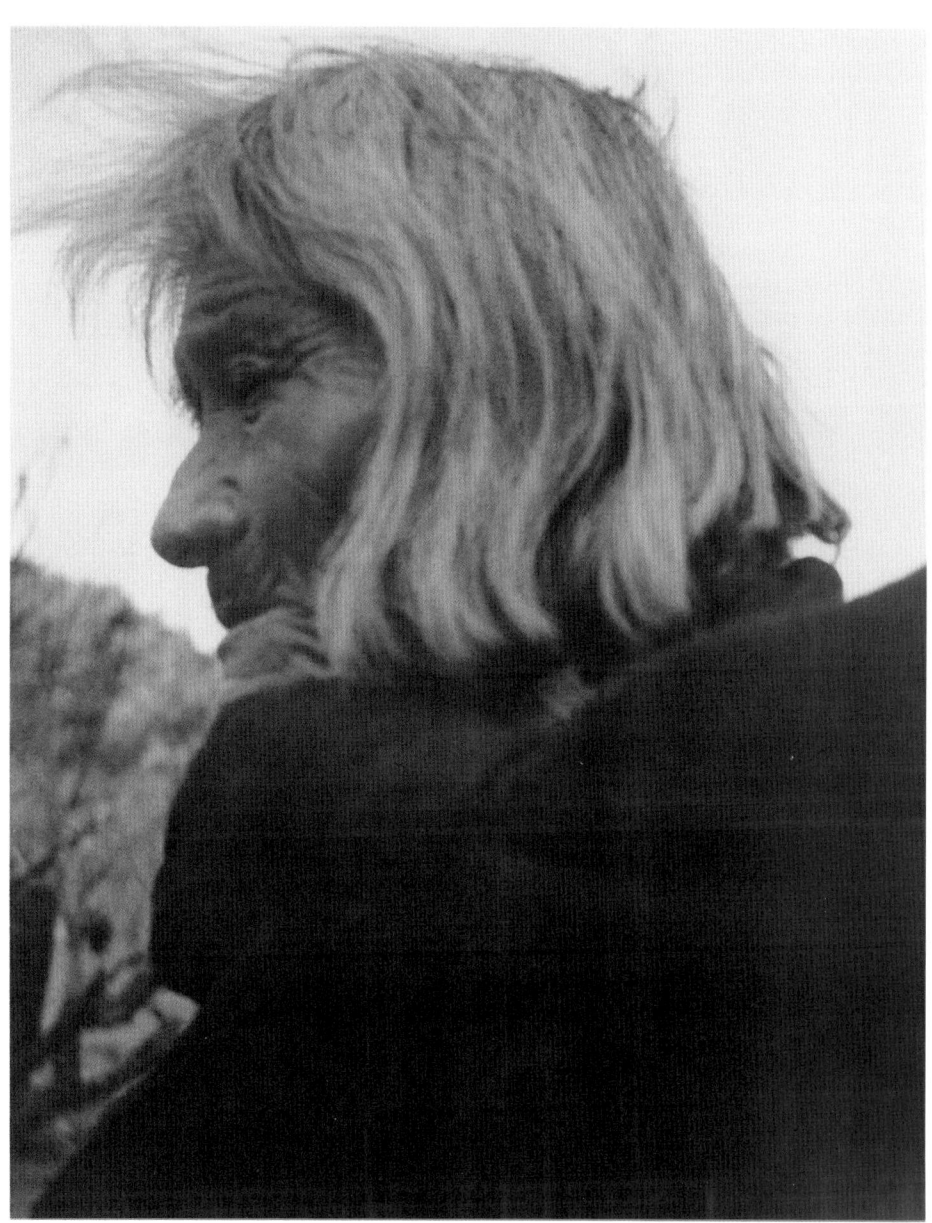

22. WIKI, WHOSE FULL NAME WAS SAMIWIKI, the Antelope priest of Walpi.

"Wiki, the genial, good-hearted old chief of the Antelope Society was one of the celebrities of Walpi. His very presence breathed benignity and his heart was full of kindness. The years were telling on Wiki, however, and the marks of age were becoming apparent in his wrinkled face. He gave one the impression of a Hopi gentleman of the old school, a survivor of the best of the past generation."

THE HOPI
Walter Hough (1915)

"News reached us of [Wiki's] death today. Wiki's wife was unkind to him. Their son had been away to school many years and had married a Pima girl and did not come home. His mother would drive Wiki out because the boy did not come home. He used to have letters written to him [at] Snake Dance time but the boy did not come. Finally she drove him out and told him to go down to Winslow and find the boy. So the poor old man took his two burros and started out, not knowing of course how he was to reach him. At Winslow he got on the track, and being deaf, did not hear the engine or of course understand the motion and was killed. Poor childish old Man."

PERSONAL DIARY
Kate Cory (1907)

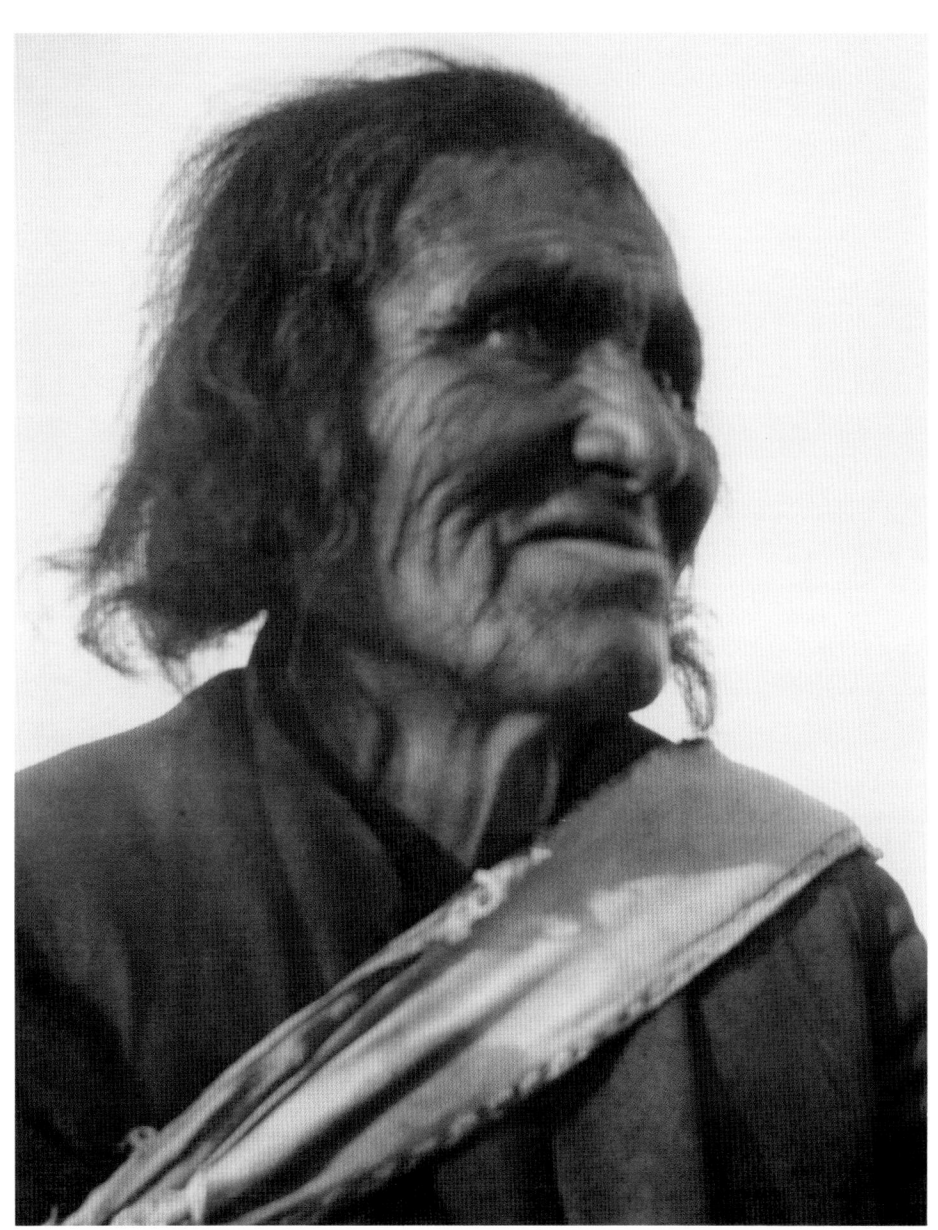

23. Kutka, a man of Walpi, sits spinning yarn.

"*So he proceeded, smoothly and deftly, while a length of spun yarn steadily took form. When a part of the yarn seemed a little thicker than the rest, he stopped the spindle and pulled the thick part out to greater length. As he resumed spinning, this part took on the right diameter and quickly assumed the proper twist.*"

Sun in the Sky
Walter O'Kane (1950)

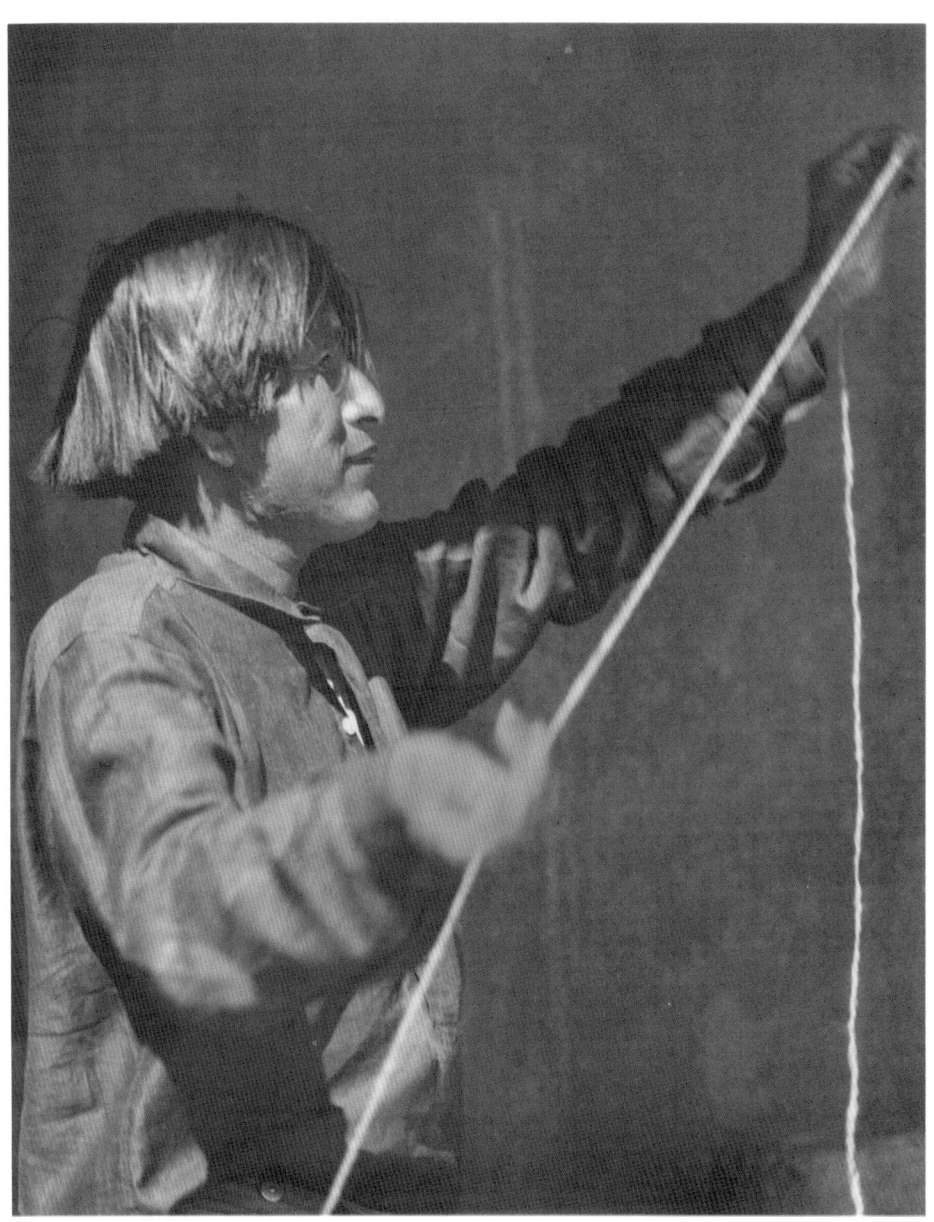

24. A Hopi man sits weaving a Navajo style of design into his blanket.

"His operations at this point were as complicated as they were swift and sure...counting across so many threads and drawing them forward, inserting a smooth stick through others, drawing the stick part way out and substituting a short piece of yarn, introducing the stick into the midst of other strands and again inserting a short length of yarn. The process was difficult to follow."

Sun in the Sky
Walter Collins O'Kane (1950)

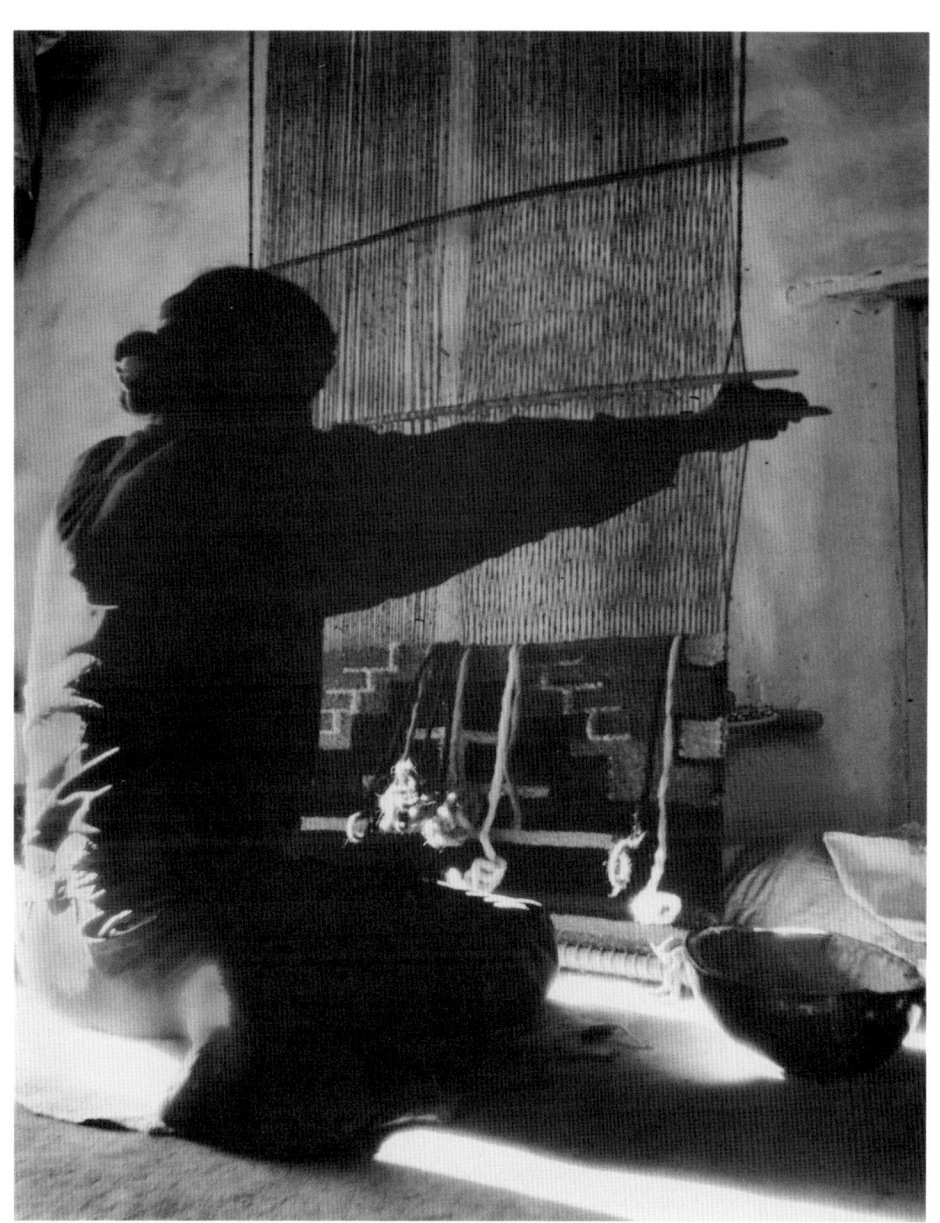

25. AN ELDERLY WOMAN TRUDGES through Kiakochomovi with a load of wood upon her back and an axe for a cane, undoubtedly on her way up the mesa to Old Oraibi from a wood-gathering trip.

"But the greatest tax is made upon the physique of the women by the heavy burdens which they carry up the mesa. The Hopi villages are situated upon the top of the mesas, which stand about six hundred feet above the plain."

NATAL CEREMONIES OF THE HOPI INDIANS
J.G. Owens (1892)

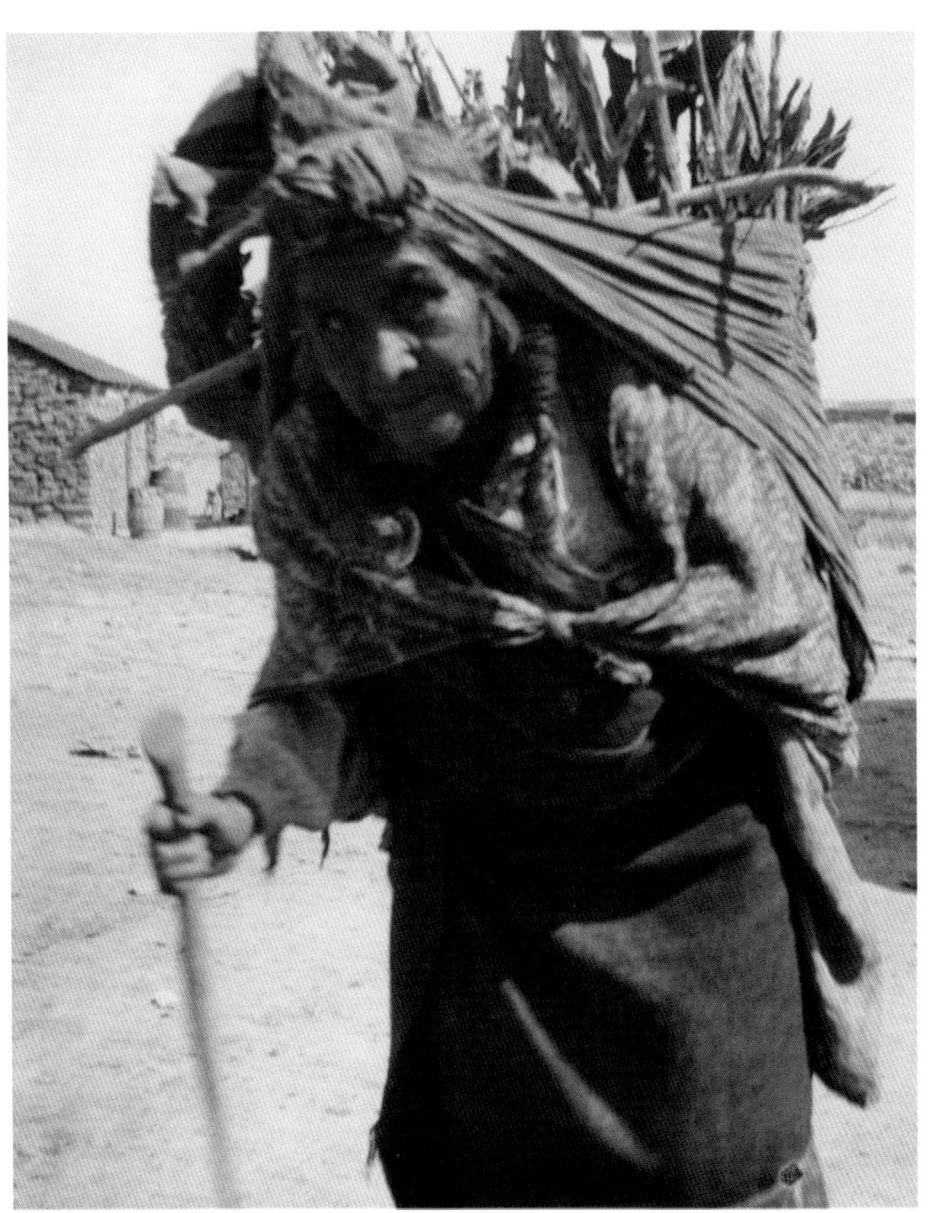

26. PORTRAIT of a Tewa man.

"A Tewa is a person born at Hano of a mother whose maternal lineage runs back unbrokenly to the original Tewa colony. There is no deviation from the rule: 'What your mother is you are.' "

HANO, A TEWA COMMUNITY IN ARIZONA
Edward P. Dozier (1966)

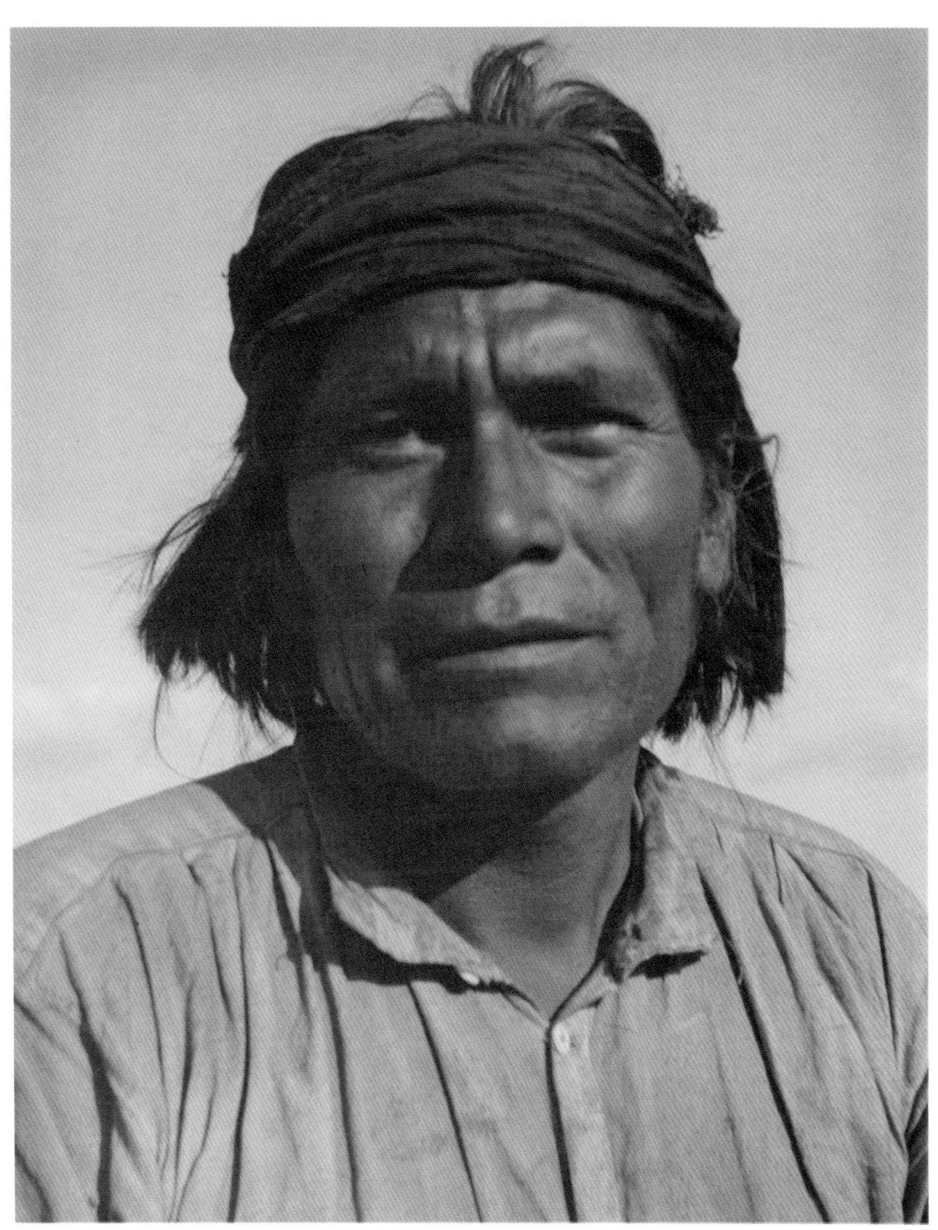

27. A Hopi woman carries water from the spring below the mesa top to her home in Sichomovi.

"All the water used, except what can be caught from melting snow in winter and from rains during the two rainy months of summer in a few small holes on the mesa top, must be carried up the mesa on the backs of the women, in jugs holding about three gallons. This is the hardest thing in the life of a Hopi woman."

NATAL CEREMONIES OF THE HOPI INDIANS
J.G. Owens (1892)

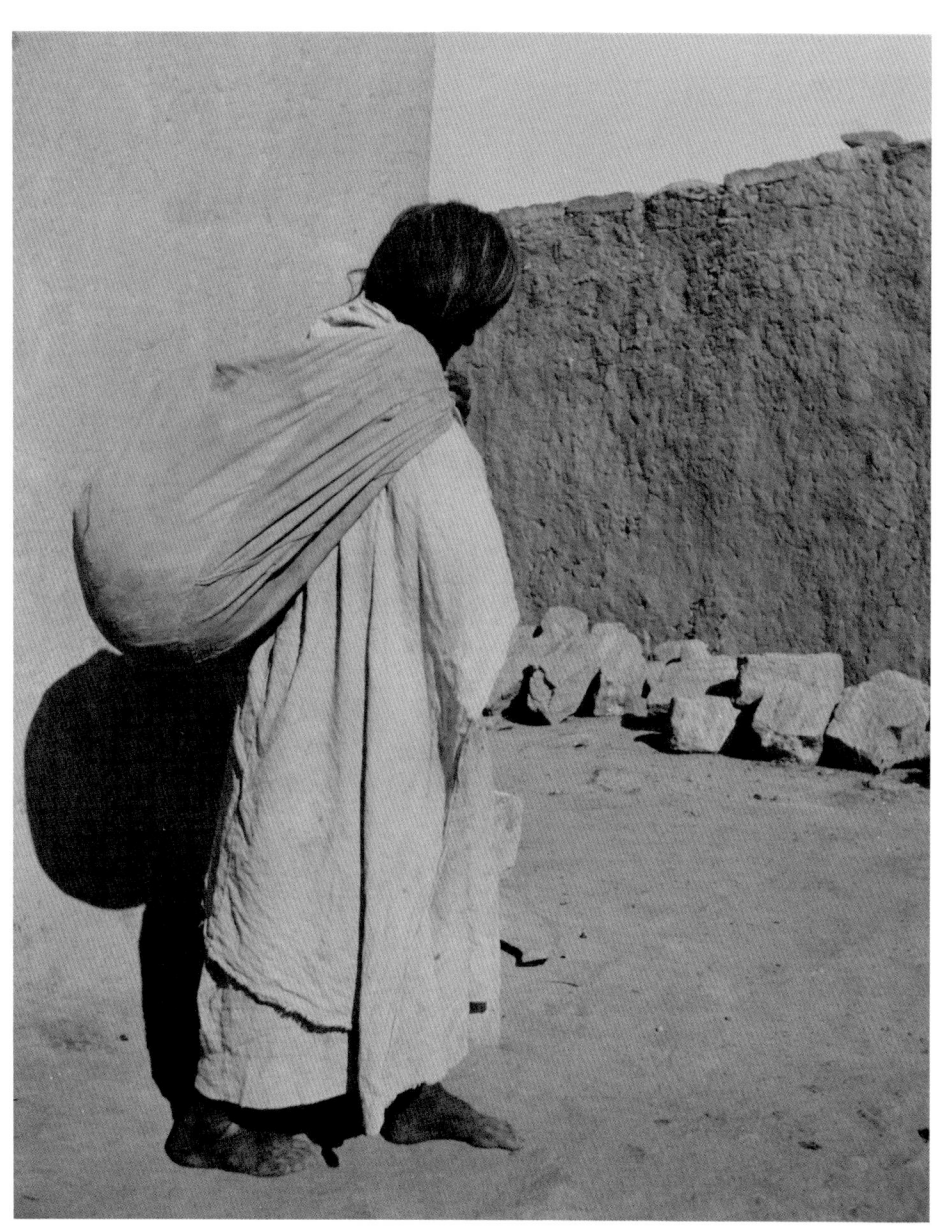

28. A YOUNG MARRIED WOMAN with corn flour on her face and her hair done in traditional dress.

"Women are like the wind, blowing first from the east and then from the west. The sooner a man learns this the better. He must expect his wife to make quick changes from joy to sadness and back to joy, in spite of anything we can do. She can be more stubborn than a mule and harder to control than either the wind or the weather."

SUN CHIEF, AUTOBIOGRAPHY OF A HOPI INDIAN

Don Talayesva from Leo Simmons (1942)

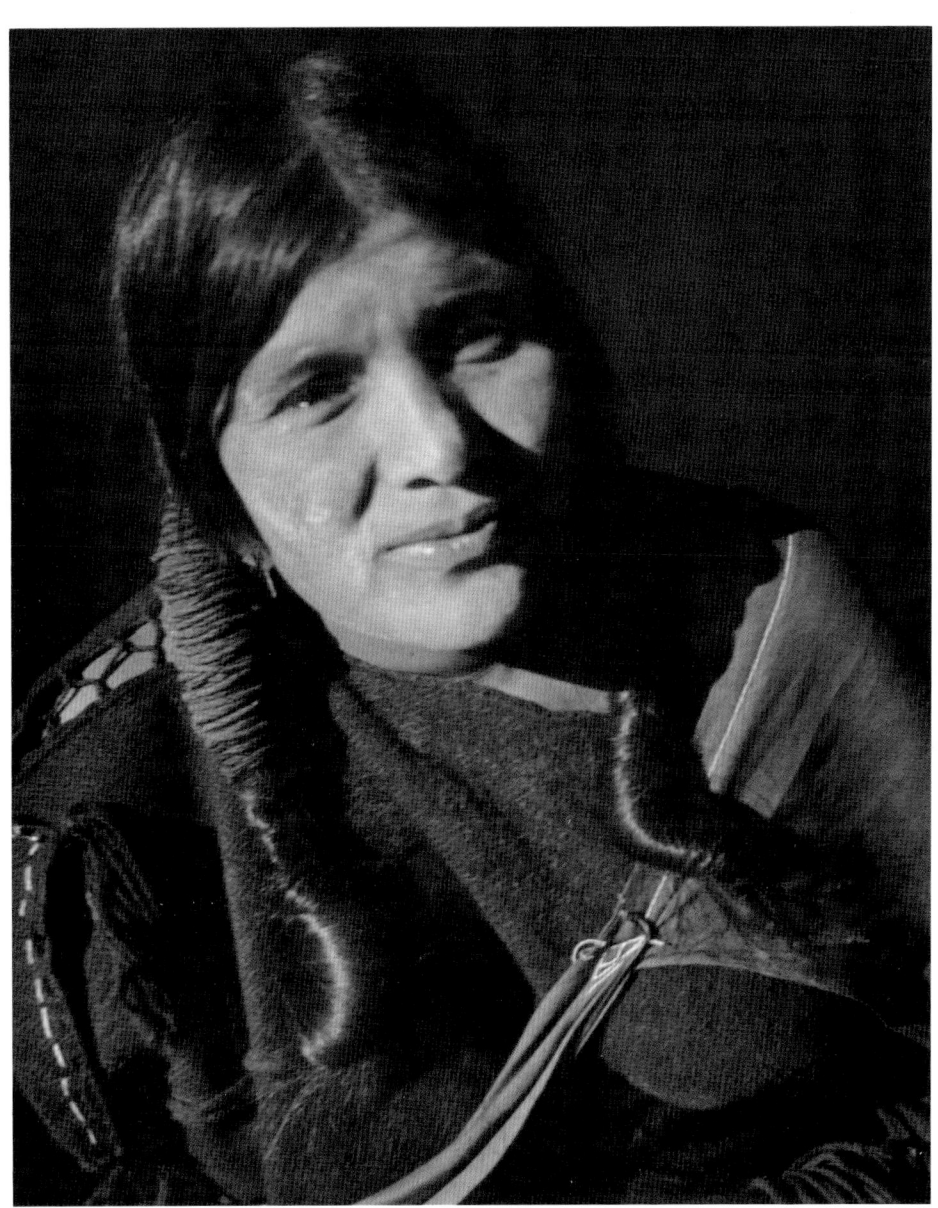

29. A Hopi portrait.

"The Hopi are a handsome people, with the classic Indian physiognomy—high cheek bones, broad noses, dark slanted eyes, full-lipped mouths. They have glossy black or dark brown hair and are generally small of stature, muscular and agile. Their skin tends to be pale reddish-brown, rather than the deeper browns and reds of other tribes."

INTRODUCTION TO THE HOPI
Paul Coze (1971)

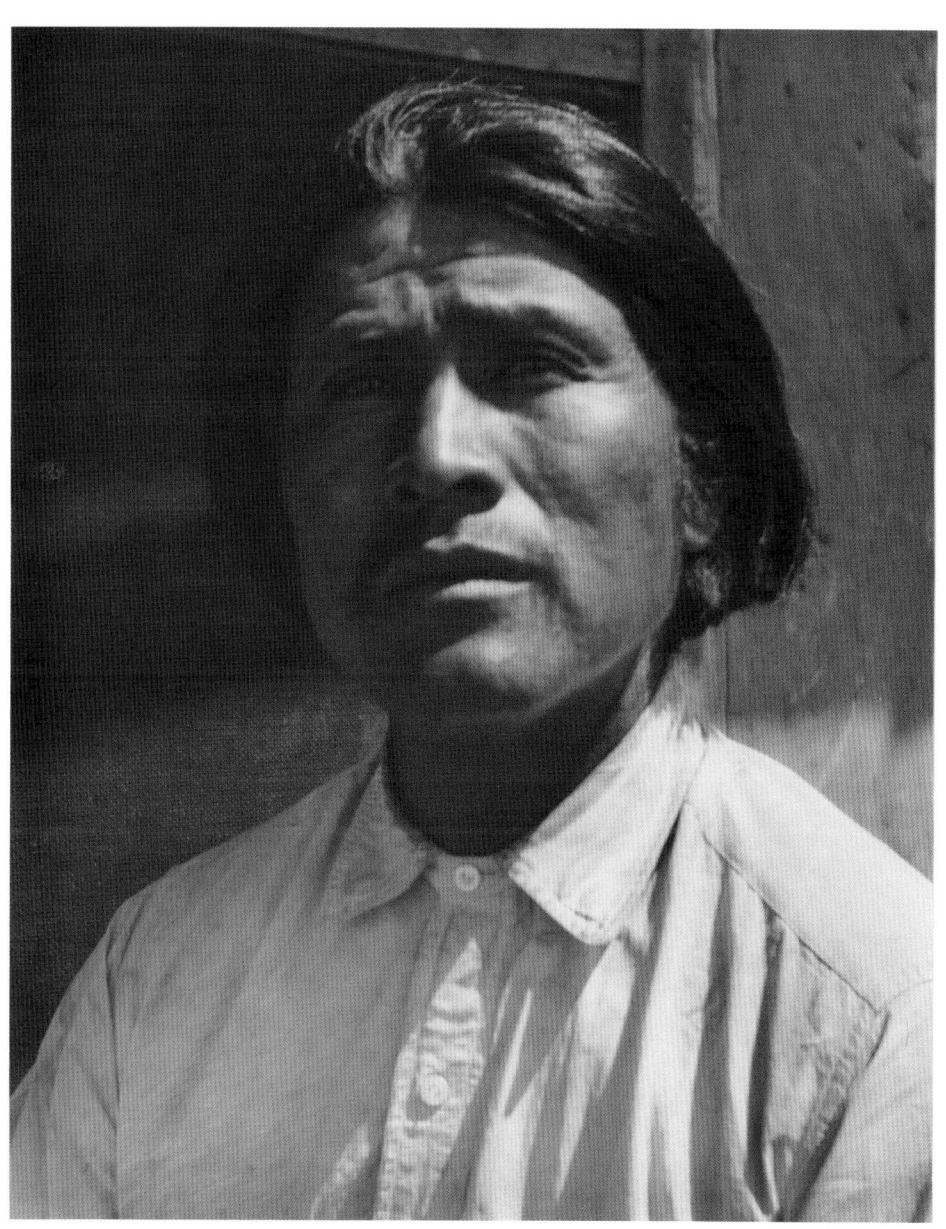

30. A Hopi portrait.

"In the Hopi view, the mother is the real head of family lineage. She is the one from whom primarily children are descended. Her blood flows in their veins. A father is respected and loved but the mother holds rank that is different in kind and degree."

SUN IN THE SKY
Walter Collins O'Kane (1950)

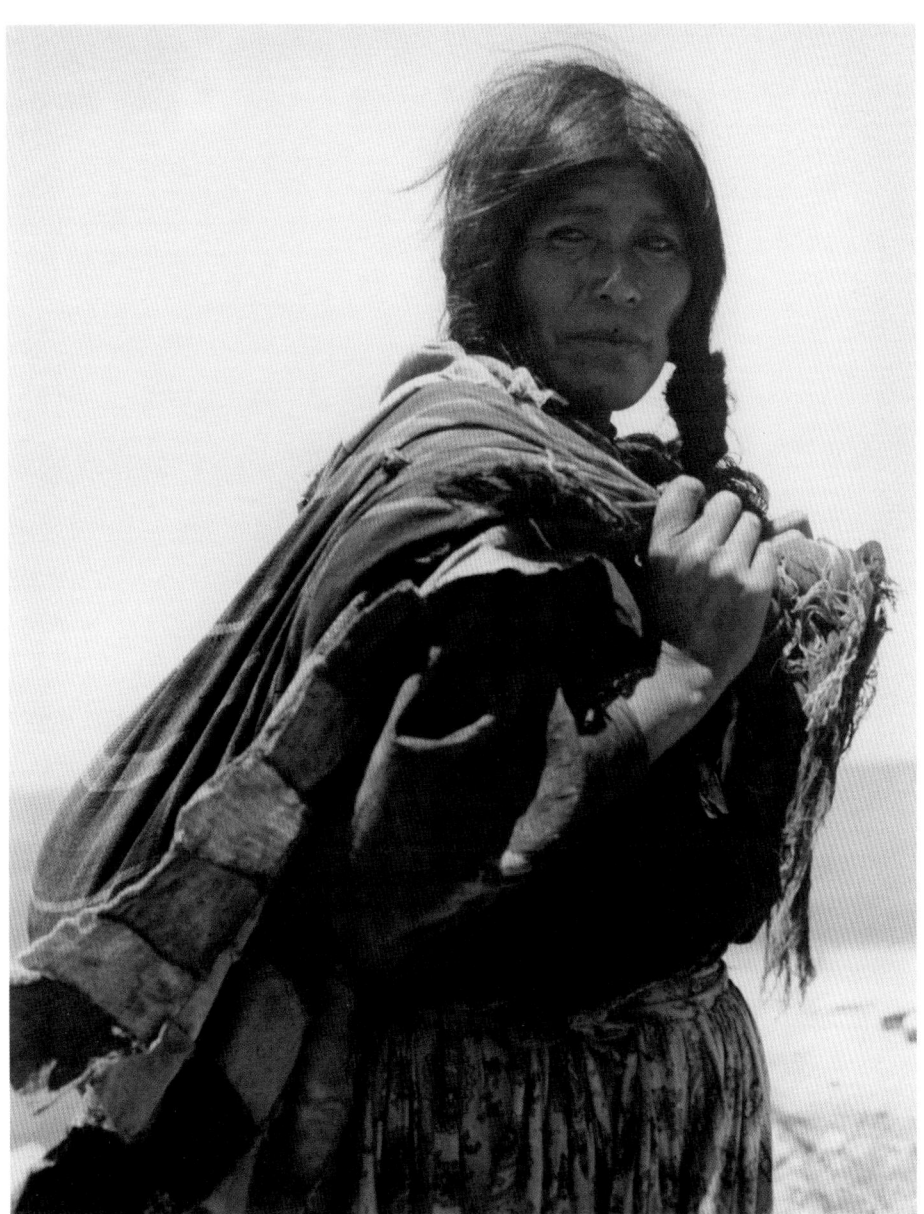

31. A HOPI MAN KNEELS in his field to break off the corn ears and put them in a blanket for transportation to the village.

"The main corn harvest begins late in September and continues the first weeks in October. Working parties are formed as for the planting and they may stay in the field from dawn till sunset. The ears are broken off in the field and carried into the villages."

HOPI AGRICULTURE AND LAND OWNERSHIP
C. Daryll Forde (1931)

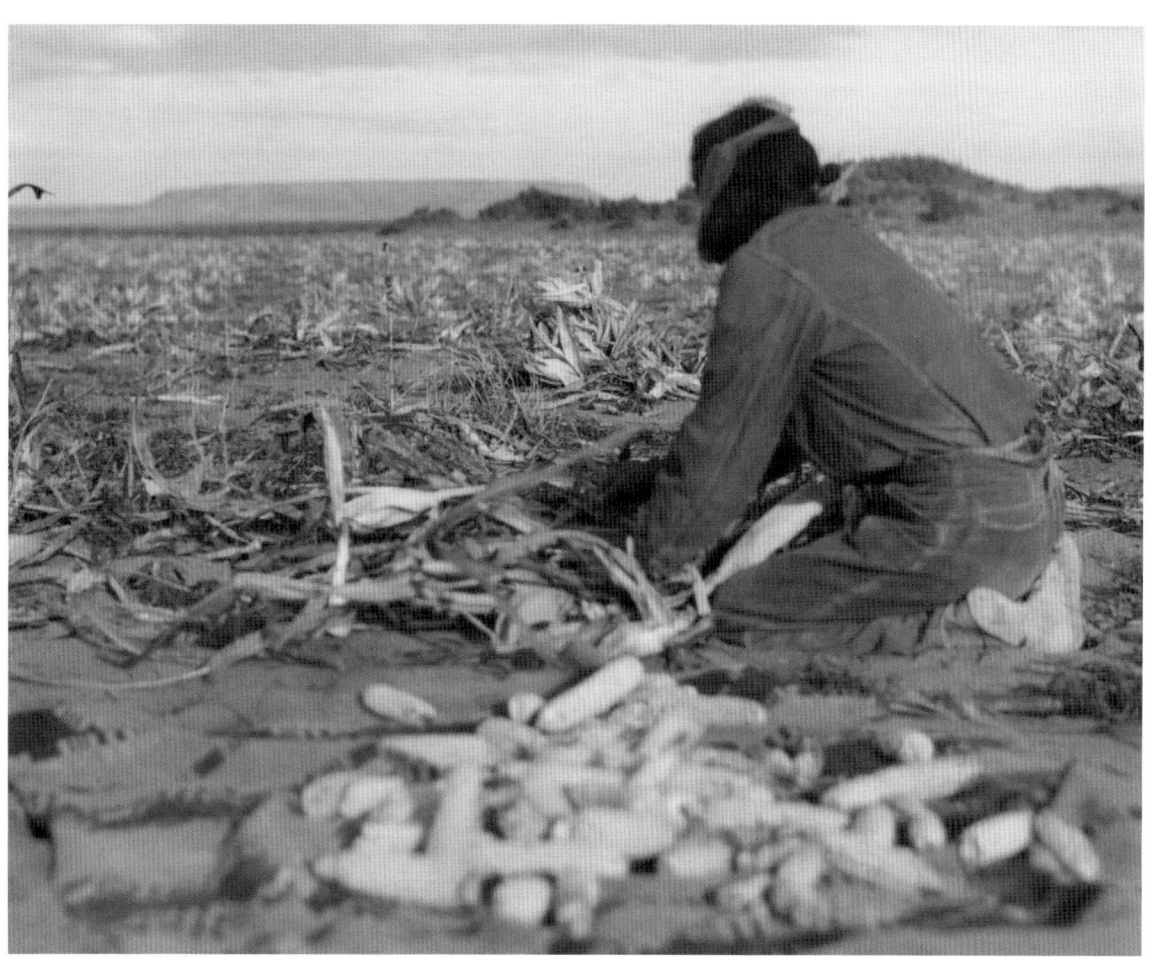

32. CORN, THE STAPLE of the Hopi, is harvested and brought in from the fields to dry upon the roof tops of the houses. A bountiful crop of corn covers the rooftops of Walpi with a carpet of color.

"No cereal in the world is so beautiful as Hopi corn. The grains, though small, are full and highly polished; the ears are white, yellow, red of several shades, a lovely rose madder, blue, a very dark blue or purple which the Hopi call black, and mottled. A tray of shelled corn looks like a mosaic."

THE HOPI INDIANS
Walter Hough (1915)

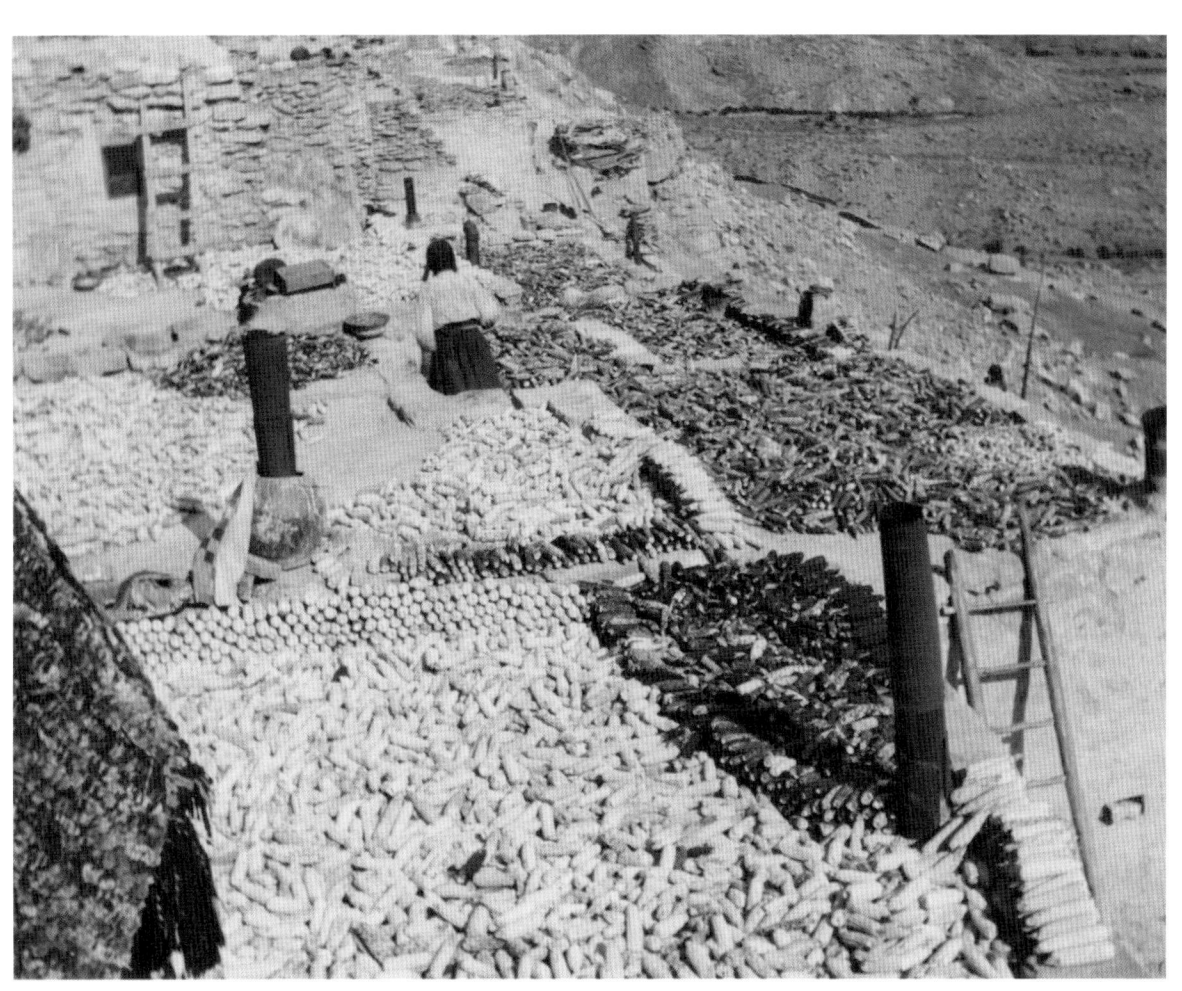

33. WOMEN AND YOUNG CHILDREN of a First Mesa household gather on a roof-top area to string corn for drying and storage.

"The household functions constantly as an economic unit; its members assist one another in daily duties and see that all are properly fed and clothed."

HANO, A TEWA COMMUNITY IN ARIZONA
Edward P. Dozier (1966)

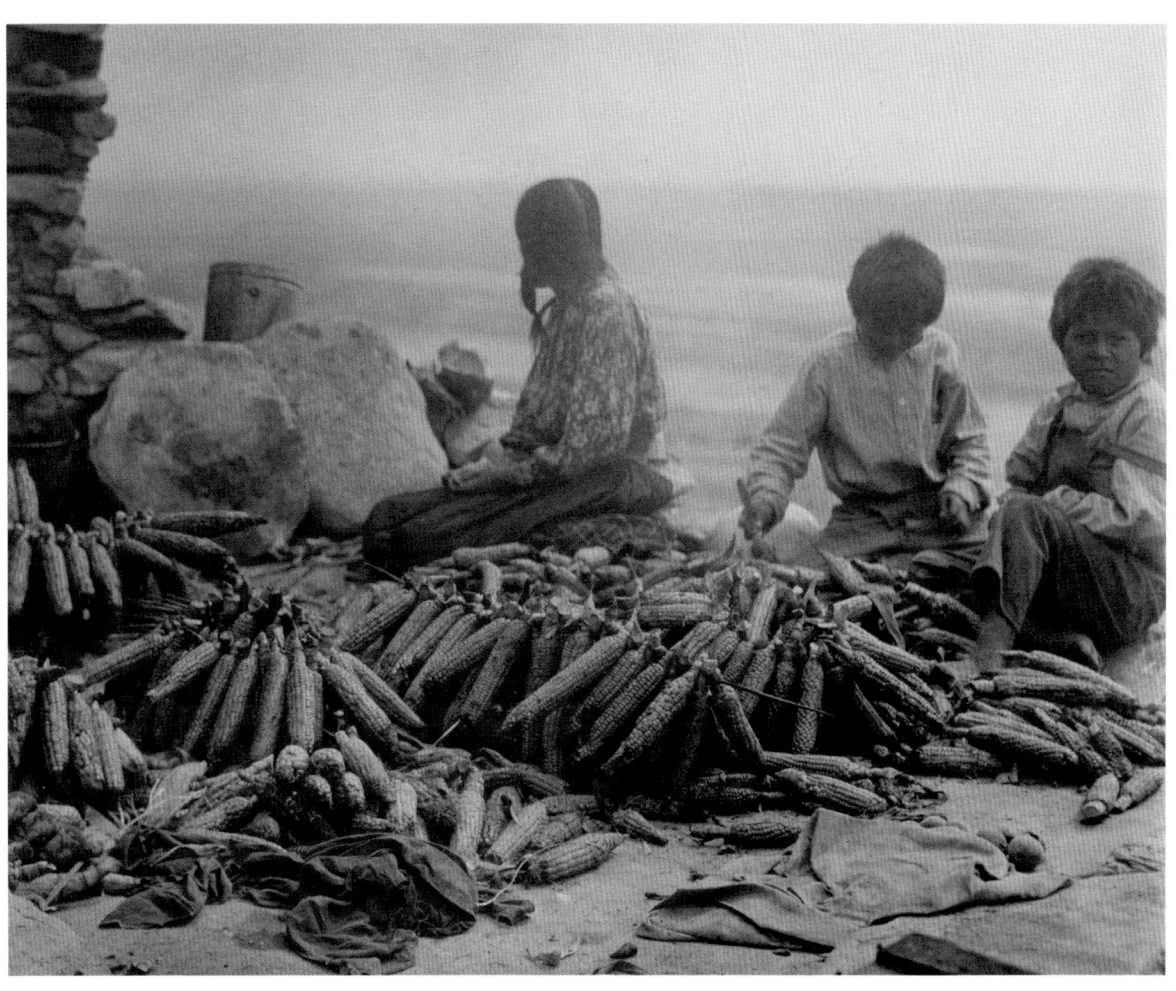

34. SHELLING CORN, the interminable routine of every Hopi woman of past years, is now done more often than not by machinery.

"*For almost every meal, corn provides the basic staple, and the preparation of meal from the corn, and its subsequent cooking, form the principal occupation of the women of the household. In the morning therefore, the woman of the house goes to her corn store and fetches a basketful of cobs. After removing the kernels and collecting them into a flat yucca fiber tray, she gets down to the serious business of grinding meal to the appropriate fineness.*"

A NATURAL HISTORY OF ASSOCIATIONS, V.II.
Maitland Bradfield (1973)

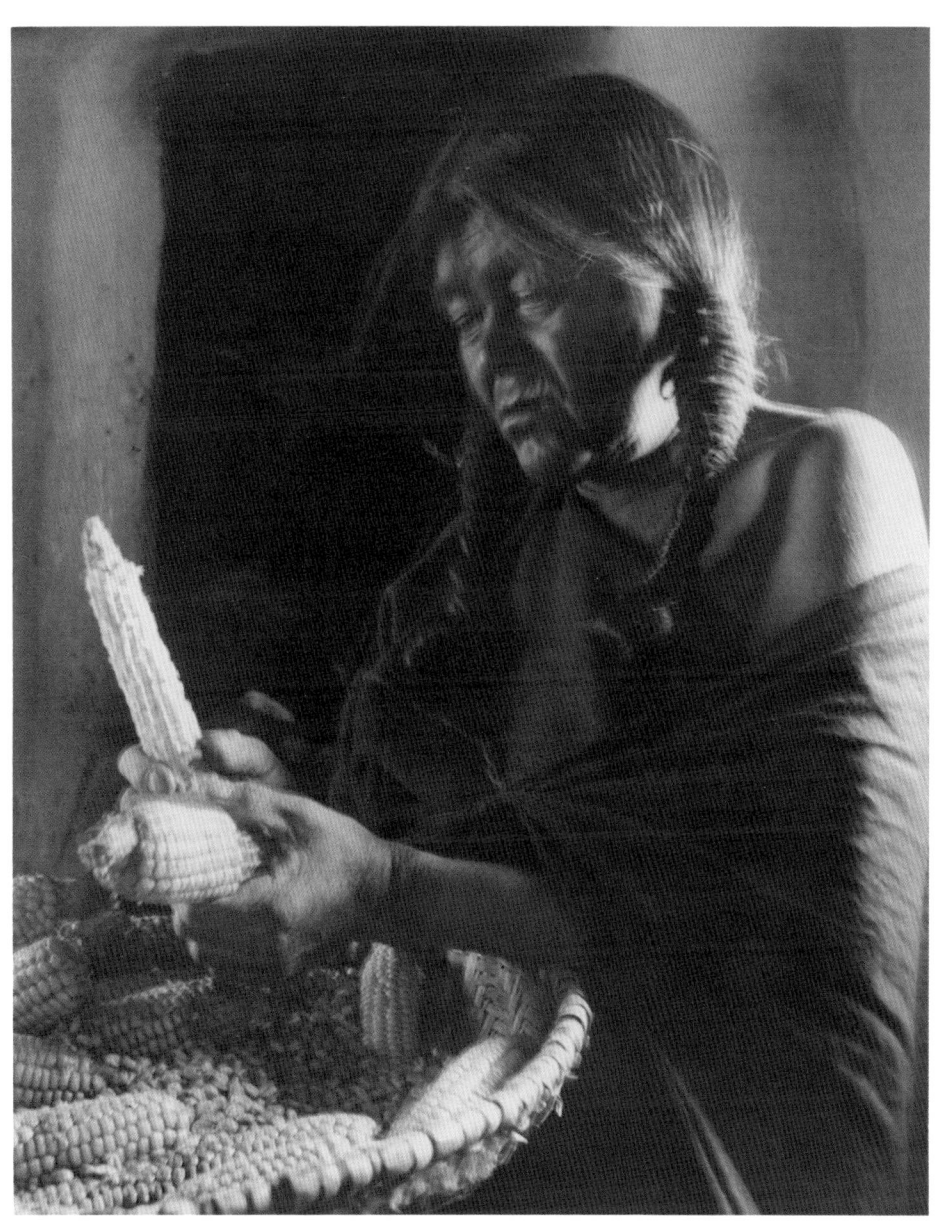

35. A Hopi woman kneels before her corner hearth making piki bread. She spreads the thin batter on a flat stone, heated to 700 degrees, with a quick swipe of her hand. The moisture in the batter prevents her hand from being burned.

"Three families are making piki to take to certain boys' houses. At the Buffalo Dance in November the boys who danced with the girls gave them presents, so now these girls are going to make a return to those boys. And all the women are helping. They will bake piki all day, and in the evening take it to the boys' houses."

Pueblo Indian Journal 1920-1921,
Introduction and Notes

Crow-Wing From Elsie Clews Parsons (1925)

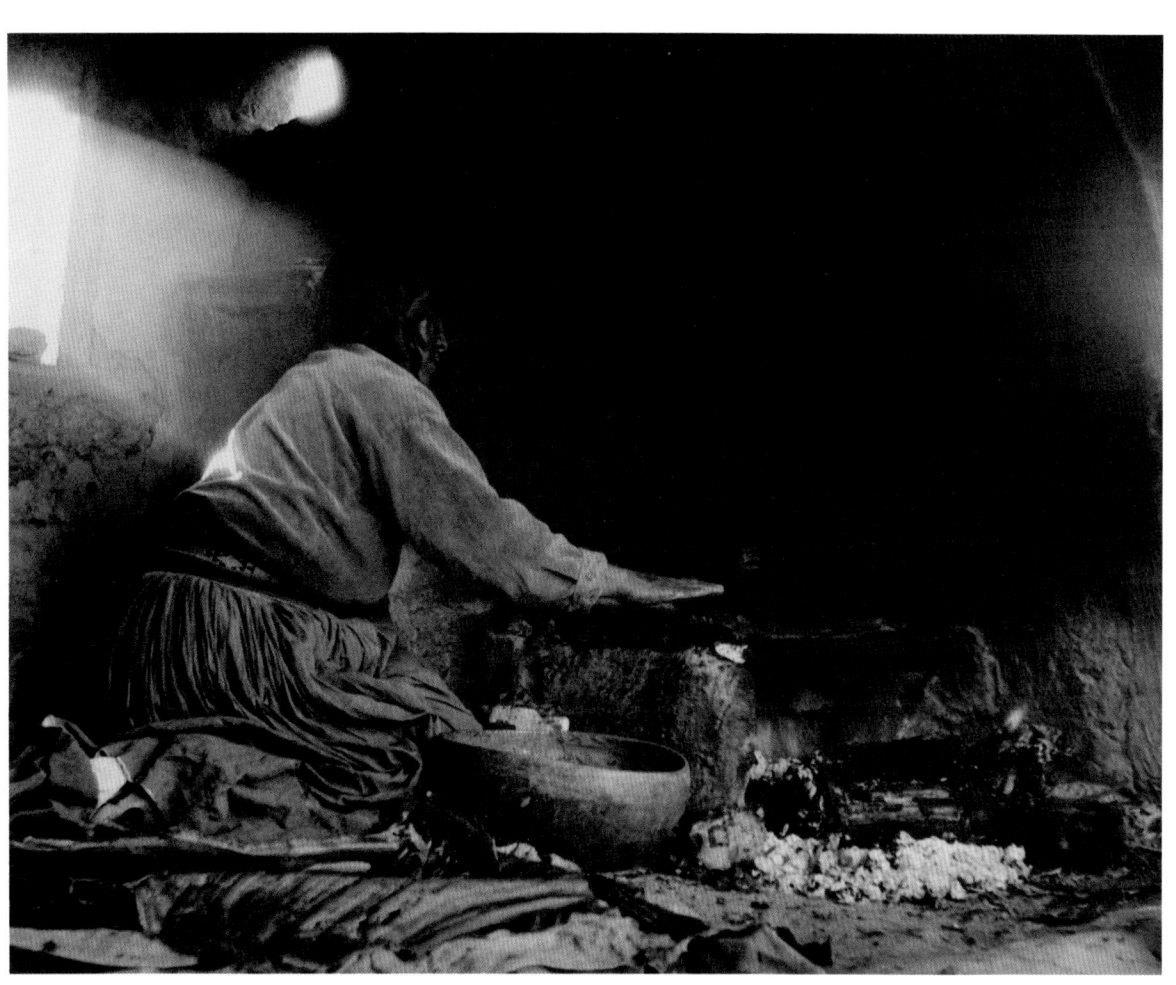

36. PROUDLY ERECT, A NAVAJO WOMAN attends a horse race at First Mesa.

"The Navaho have been neighbors of the Hopi villages for a long time. About [and during the] 200 years prior to their removal to Eastern New Mexico they constantly raided and plundered Hopi fields and threatened the lives of the villagers. The Tewa and Hopi enjoyed a brief respite from the Navaho menace, but a few years after being returned to their native land, problems with the Navaho again appeared."

HANO, A TEWA COMMUNITY IN ARIZONA
Edward P. Dozier (1966)

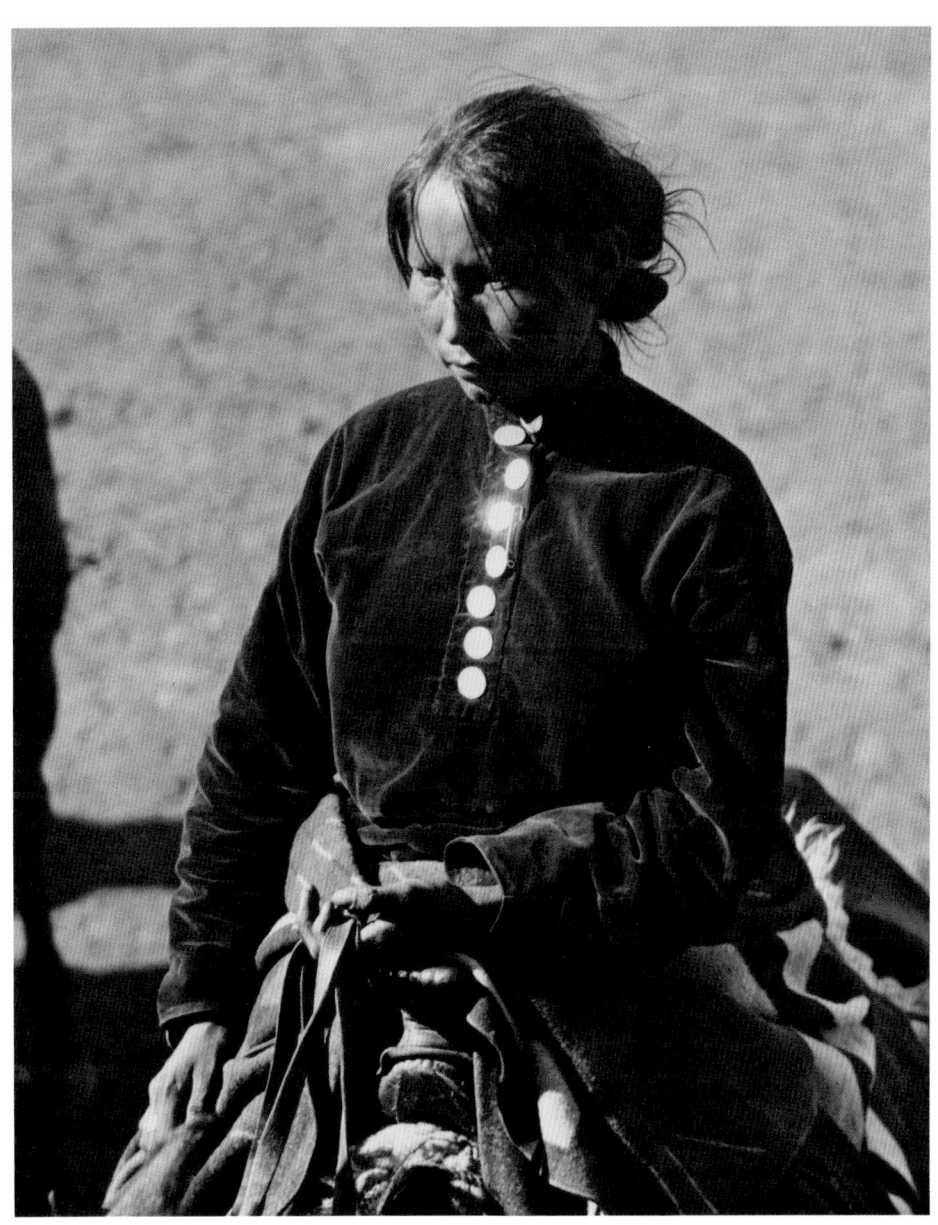

37. THESE YOUNG HOPI HORSEMEN are dressed in the fashion of their non-Indian contemporaries of the same age and era.

"The mature Hopi has a thick figure, not inclined to fatness, but with barrel-like lungs and a sturdy back. He would make a fine wrestler. As he has accepted things of civilization via the trader...his costume is not radically different today. The curious dresses of the olden-time, of buckskin, cloth of native weave, and feathers, such as may be seen in the Harvey collection at Albuquerque, have disappeared from the mesas and to the younger generation are unknown."

INDIANS OF THE ENCHANTED DESERT
Leo Crane (1925)

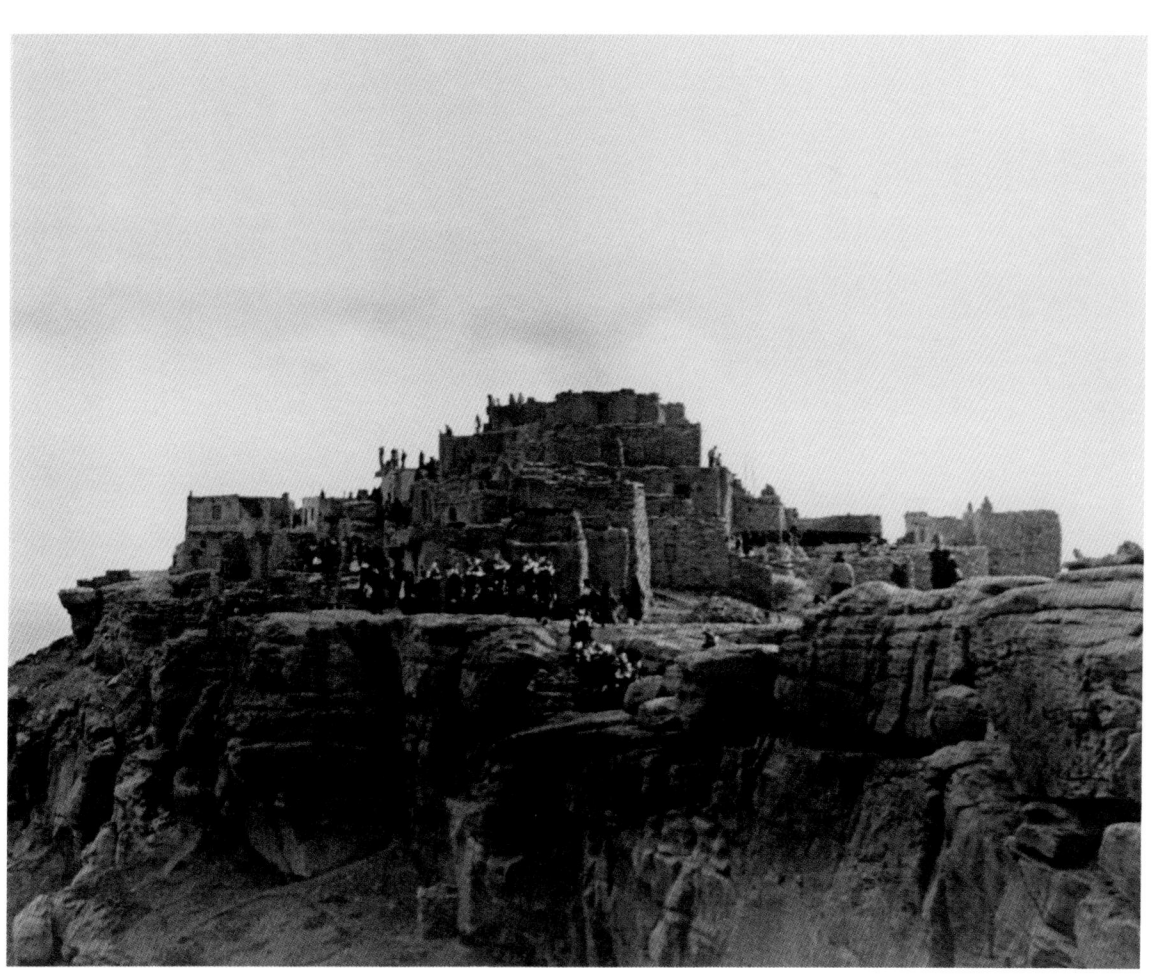

39. THE HEMIS KACHINAS SING facing the kneeling Kachin'manas who accompany them with gourd and rasper. Kachina priests hover behind to make sure that all is in order.

"...there's a time when the kachinas enter the plaza with their arms full of fresh green corn, ears still on the stalks, and melons. Sprigs of evergreen from the San Francisco Peaks form a dense collar on each figure, and branches hang down from their waists. As the kachinas lay down their gifts the rustle of corn leaves and a fresh green smell fill the plaza..."

FRED KABOTIE, HOPI INDIAN ARTIST
Fred Kabotie from Bill Belknap (1977)

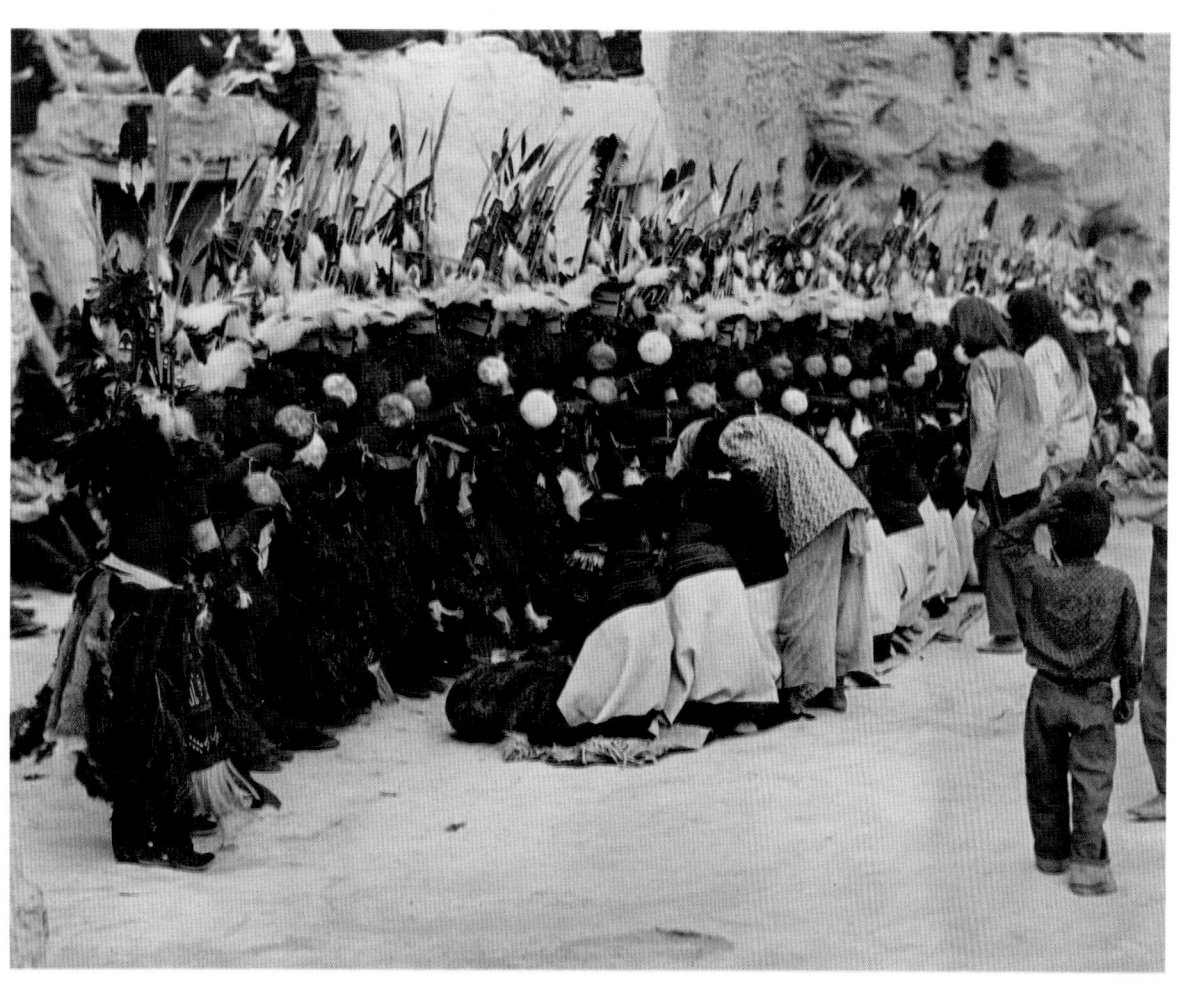

40. THE HEMIS KACHINA IS A FAVORITE impersonation for the Niman Ceremony. This is the time when the kachinas return to their home on the San Francisco Peaks where they will remain for six months, making rain for the crops of the Hopi, until they return once again. Flanked by the Kachin' Manas, the line of Hemis Kachina are led to a new dance position in Oraibi plaza by the kachina fathers.

"At the time of the Niman ceremony in the Hopi villages, elaborate altars are erected in the kivas, or underground chambers, before which sacred rites are performed and songs are sung. It is especially on this occasion that the men make toys for the children—Kachina dolls for the girls, and bows and arrows for the boys. On the last day of the ceremony, which occupies altogether about a fortnight, the Kachinas bring great quantities of corn, beans, melon, and peaches, which are distributed among the people, especially the children—literally fruits from the gods."

THE KACHINAS ARE COMING
Gene Meany Hodge (1936)

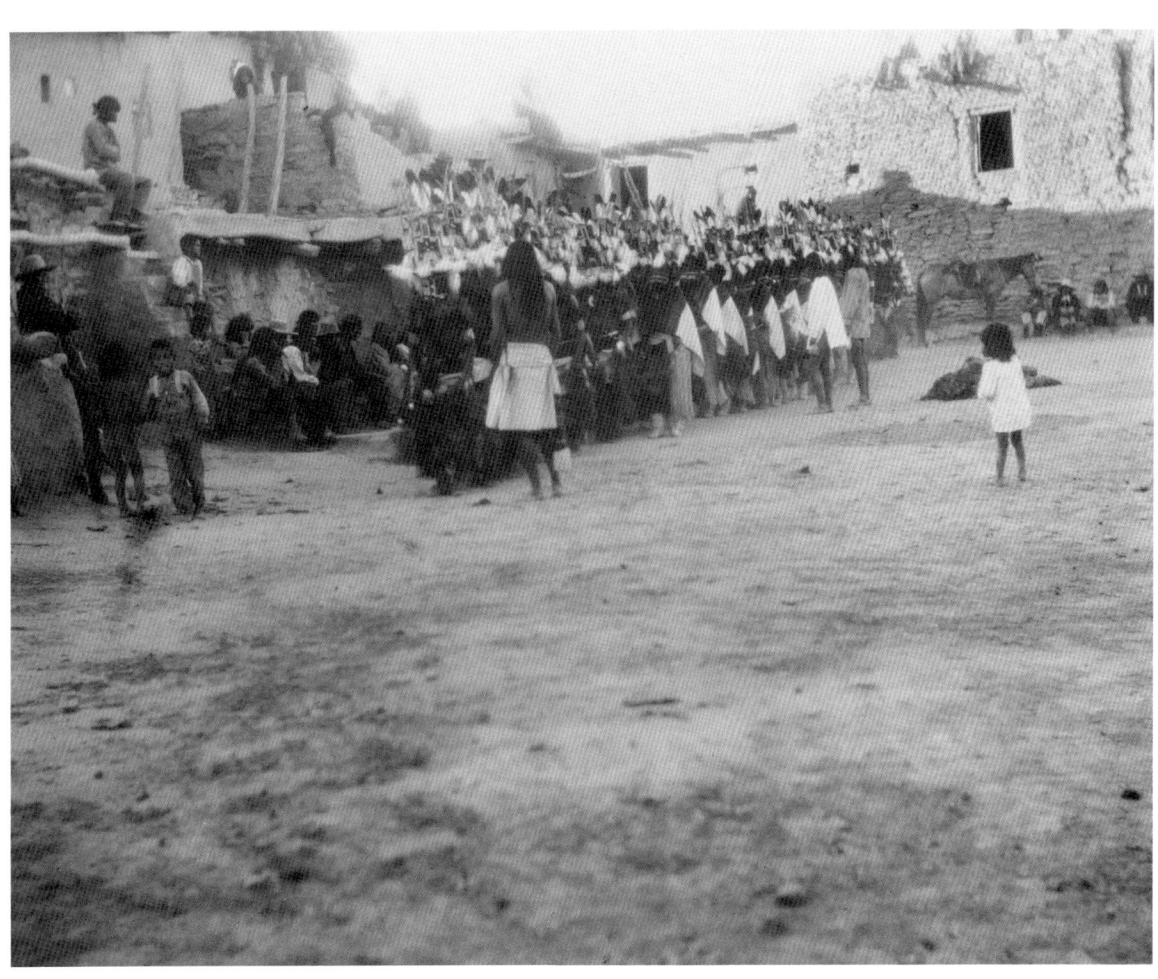

41. THE HEMIS OR HOME-GOING KACHINAS gather in the plaza at Walpi with their gifts of corn before dancing.

"It is a farewell of beautiful, barbaric pageantry. There are helmet masks topped with feathers and grass. High terraced tablitas are painted with cloud and rainbow, with corn and butterfly, sometimes on the back a kachina doll standing on an ear of corn. The inevitable ruff of spruce around the throat, a sprig carried in one hand."

MASKED GODS
Frank Waters (1950)

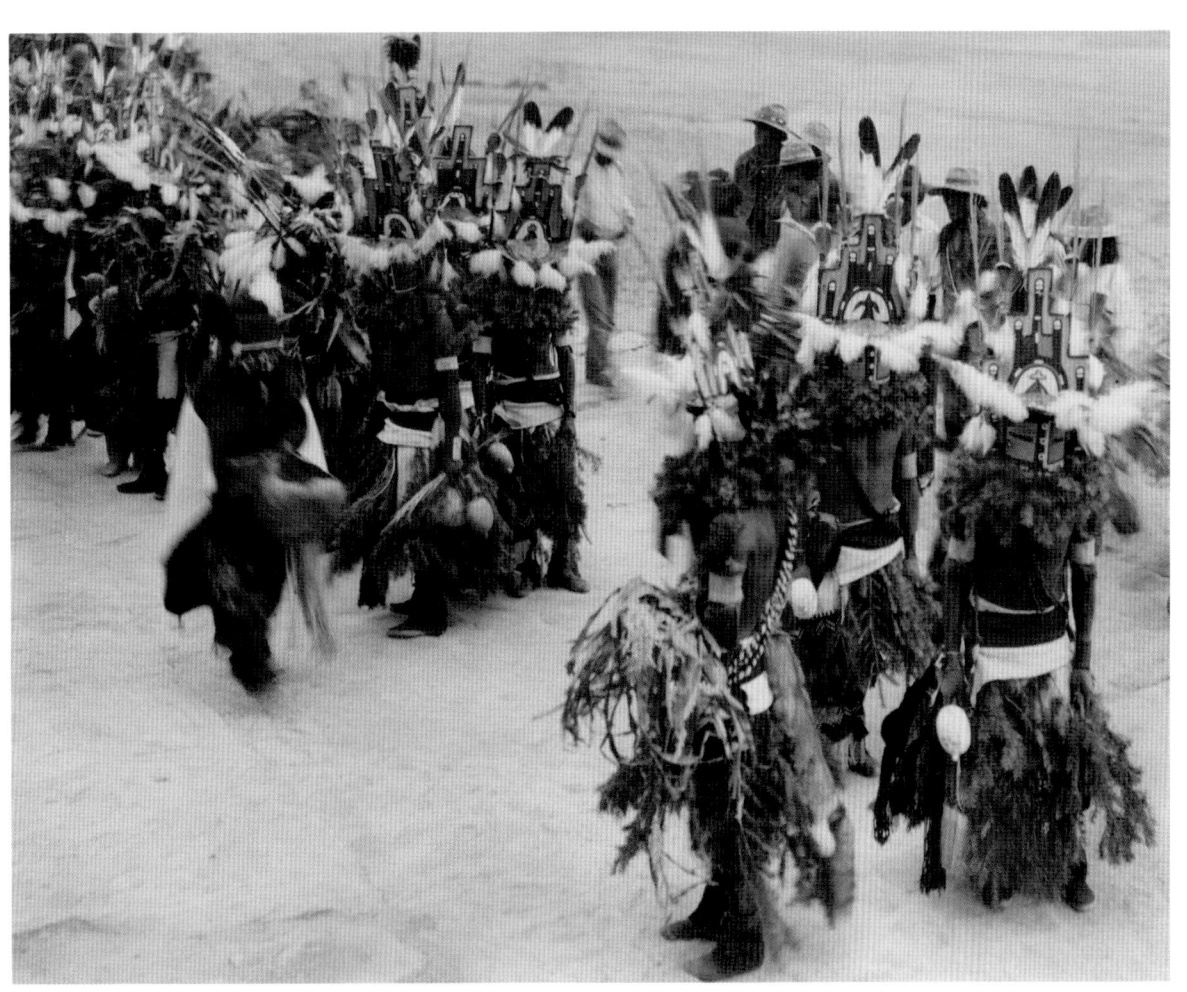

42. ONE OF THE NIMAN DANCERS, a Hemis Kachina, holds forth a bow and arrows for some small boy in the cluster of onlookers. The gift is unusual in that it has a small kachina doll attached to it.

"Usually the kachina dancers bring various gifts on their first entrance, which they place in the center of the kisonvi (plaza). At the completion of the third song-set, the dancers break ranks and distribute the gifts to the spectators before leaving for their rest-period. These gifts are either from the kachina impersonators or from non-participants who have requested a dancer to give an article in their behalf."

THE KACHINA AND THE WHITE MAN
Frederick J. Dockstader (1954)

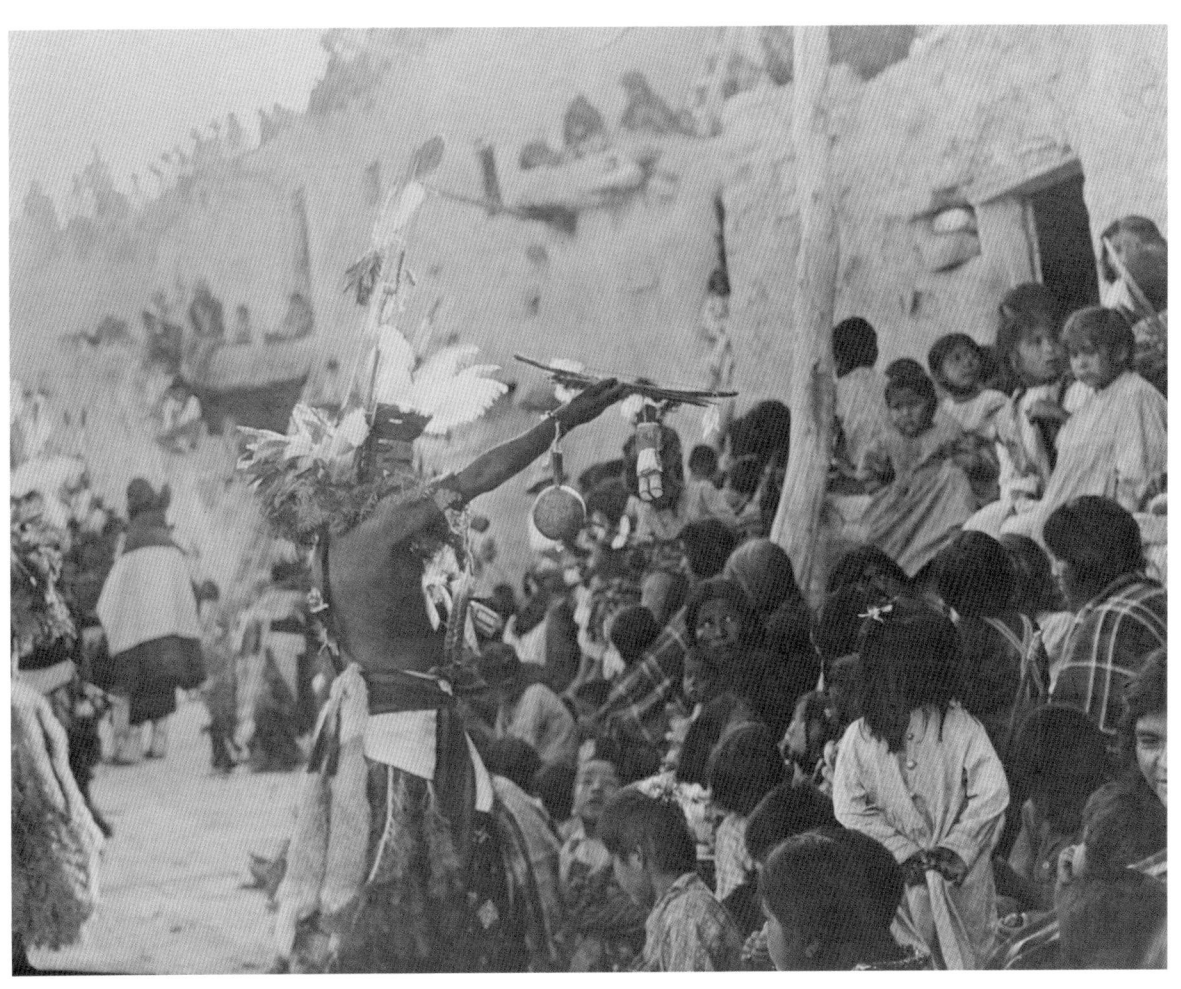

43. AS SPECTATORS LINE THE ROOFS the men and women of the Powamu Society gather to cast their prayer meal upon the kachinas and to give their messages that rain is needed for the crops. The Hemis Kachinas who have danced in the Niman Ceremony will take this message to the rain beings as they go home to the San Francisco Peaks.

"Toward evening, they are led to the kiva in which the altar has been set up. Here they dance for the last time. When they have finished, members of the Powamu society, both men and women, dressed in kilts and sashes or ceremonial robes, emerge from the kiva. One smokes upon each kachina, another sprinkles each with medicine, and the others place prayer sticks and sacred meal in their left hands."

HOPI KACHINAS
Edwin Earle and Edward A. Kennard (1938)

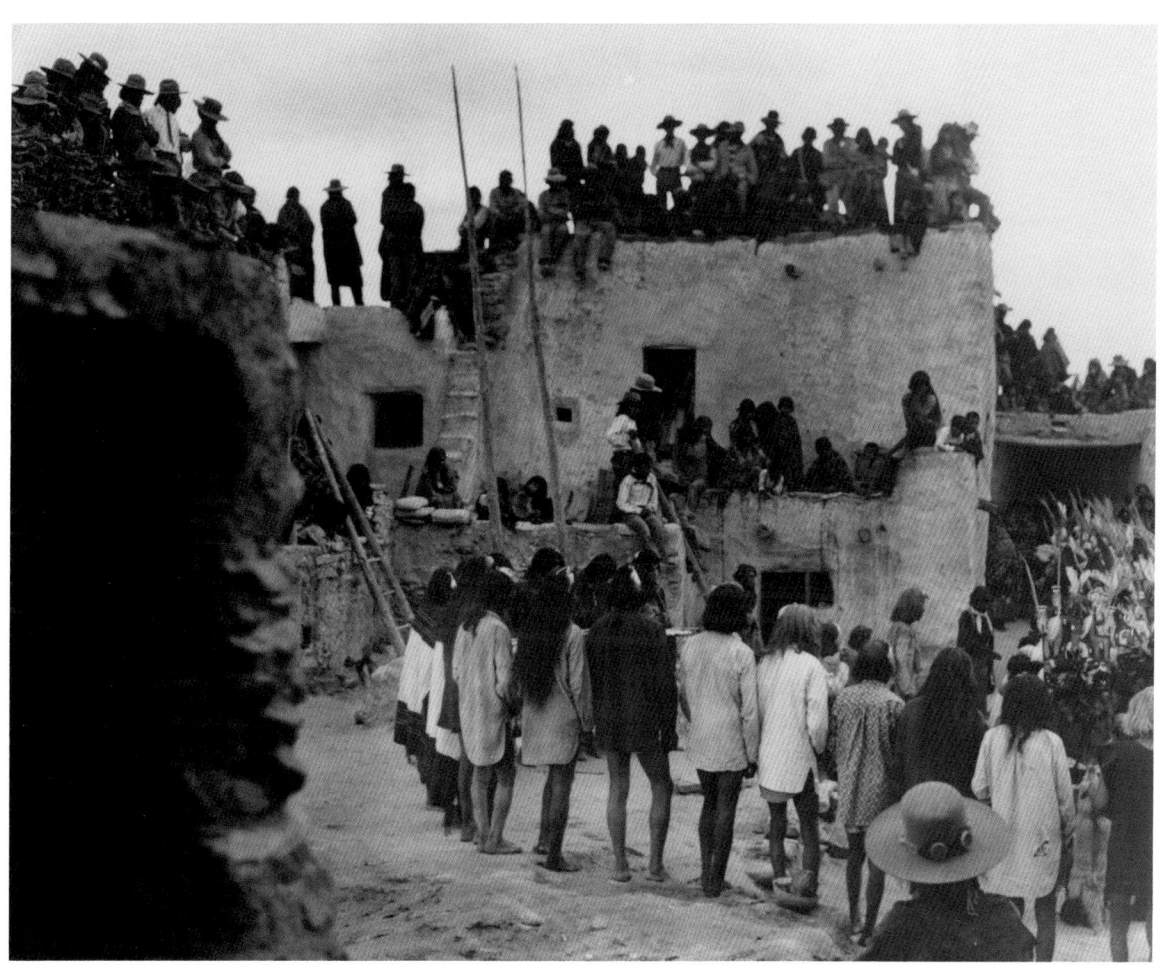

44. THE PRINCIPALS IN THE NIMAN CEREMONY of late July cluster about the entrance to the Chief Kiva at Walpi. The hatchway is marked with cloud patterns and an important ritual takes place as the kachinas stand two by two on the sides of the kiva.

"The kachina come this morning just after the sun comes up. Eototo goes first and then the other kachina follow him. —Coyote clan man and Flute man stand on the north side; on the east side stand Bear clan man and Snake clan man; Patki clan man and Rabbit clan man stand on the south side; on the west side stand Reed Clan and Horn clan man. In an hour Powamu men and women will all come out of the kiva; then the Powamu chief will be ahead and all of the kachina will follow him."

PUEBLO INDIAN JOURNAL 1920-21,
INTRODUCTION AND NOTES

Crow-Wing from Elsie Clews Parsons (1925)

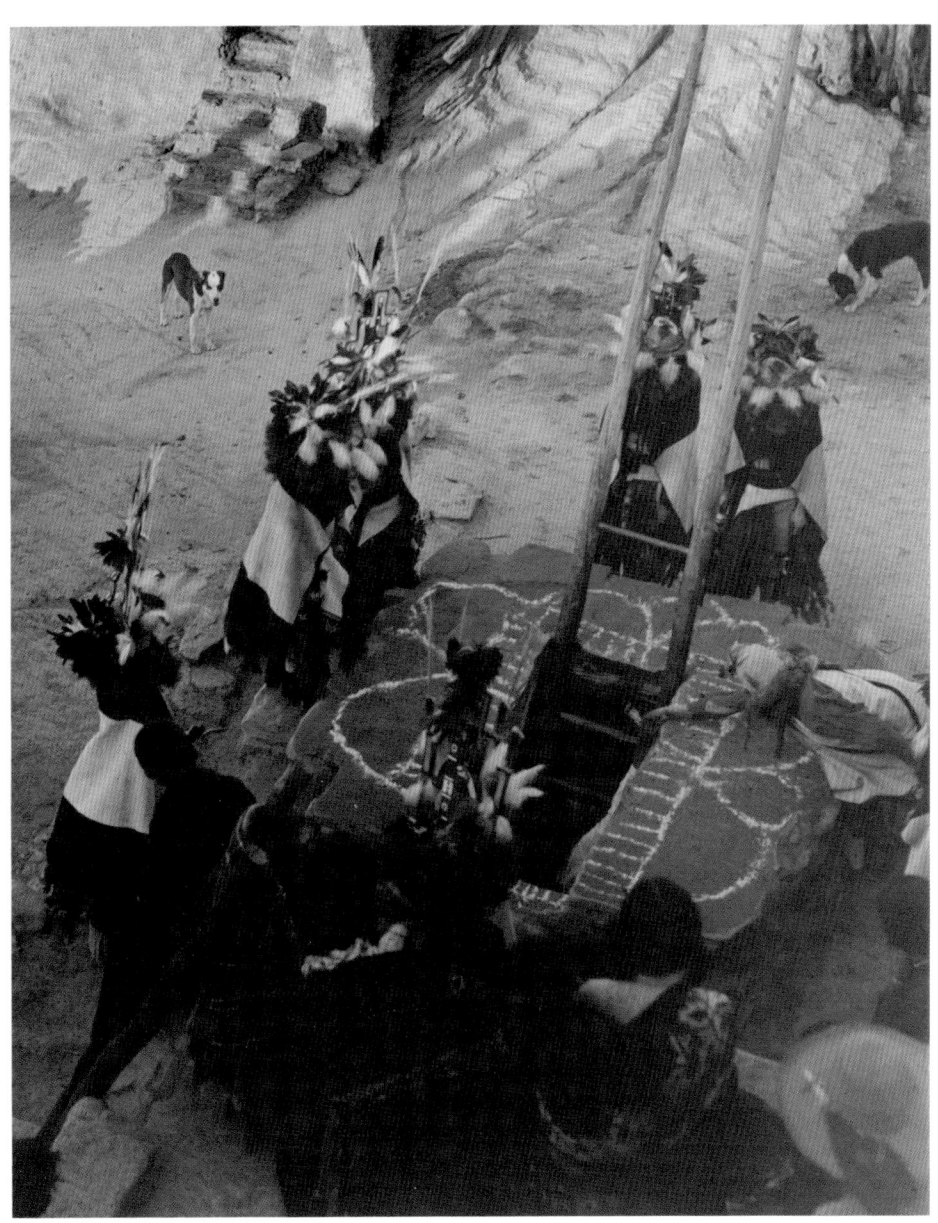

45. THE KACHINA CHIEF BEARING the thorn bush leads the ritual circuit of Eototo, Kachin' Mana and the Hemis Kachinas about the cloud-decorated hatchway of the Chief Kiva at Walpi. He passes a row of Powamu Manas who sprinkle prayer meal on the kachinas as they pass. An audience of small children crowd an adjoining roof to watch.

"From Kowawaima come four couples of Hümis Kachina arrayed as yesterday, but with the addition of red and blue bordered blankets and their bodies whitened. There are six Hümis, one Ma'lo, and Eo'toto. Ma'lo stands on the northwest and carries the box-thorn."

HOPI JOURNAL
Alexander M. Stephen (1936)

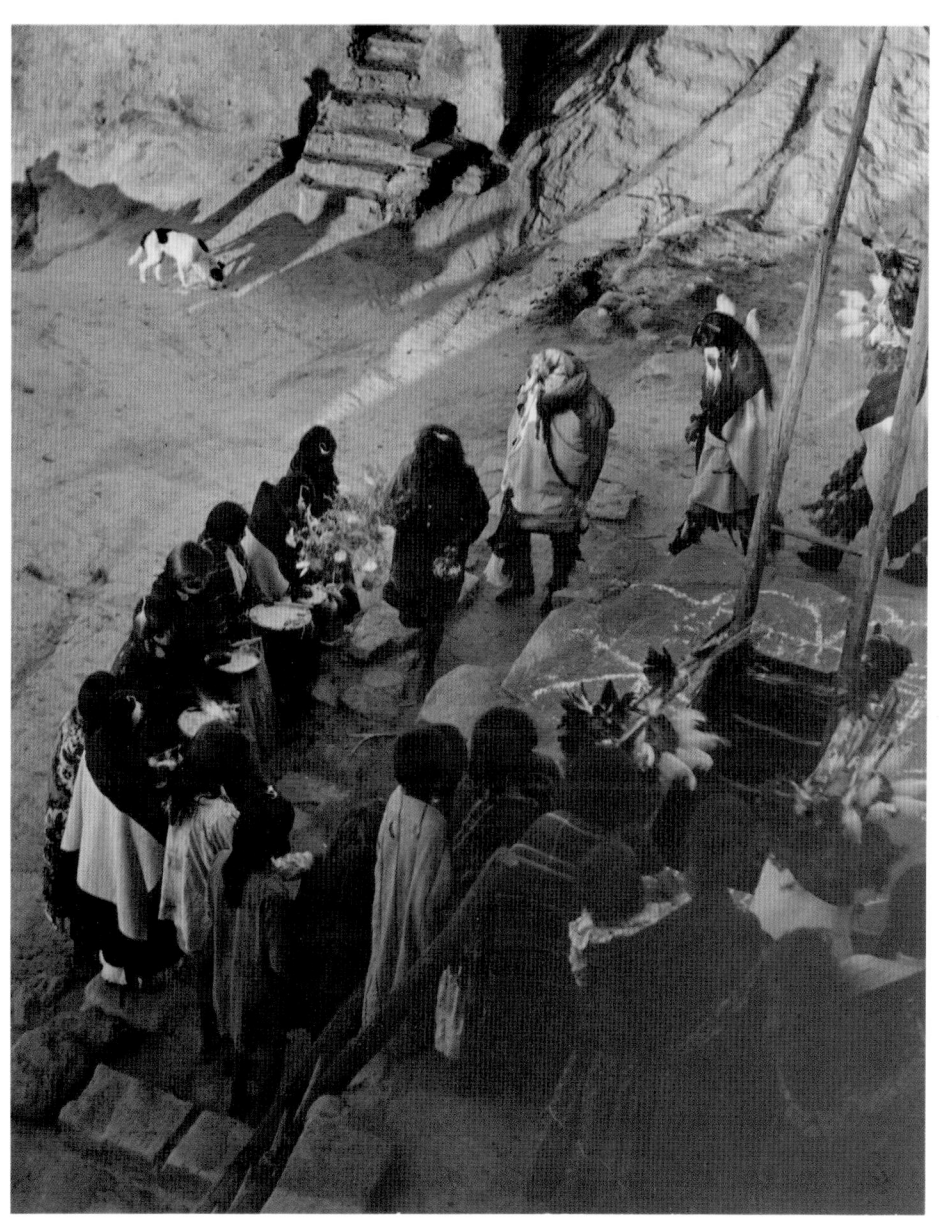

46. IN THE PRELIMINARY VIOLENCE that led to the division of Old Oraibi in 1906, three Hopi men struggle outside of a house.

"Thereupon, the Friendlies set about clearing the village of Shungopovis. They began at the very spot where they stood; but every Friendly who laid hold of a Shungopovi to put him out of doors was attacked from behind by an Oraibi Hostile, so that the three went wrestling and struggling out of doors together."

ME AND MINE
Helen Sekaquaptewa from Louise Udall (1969)

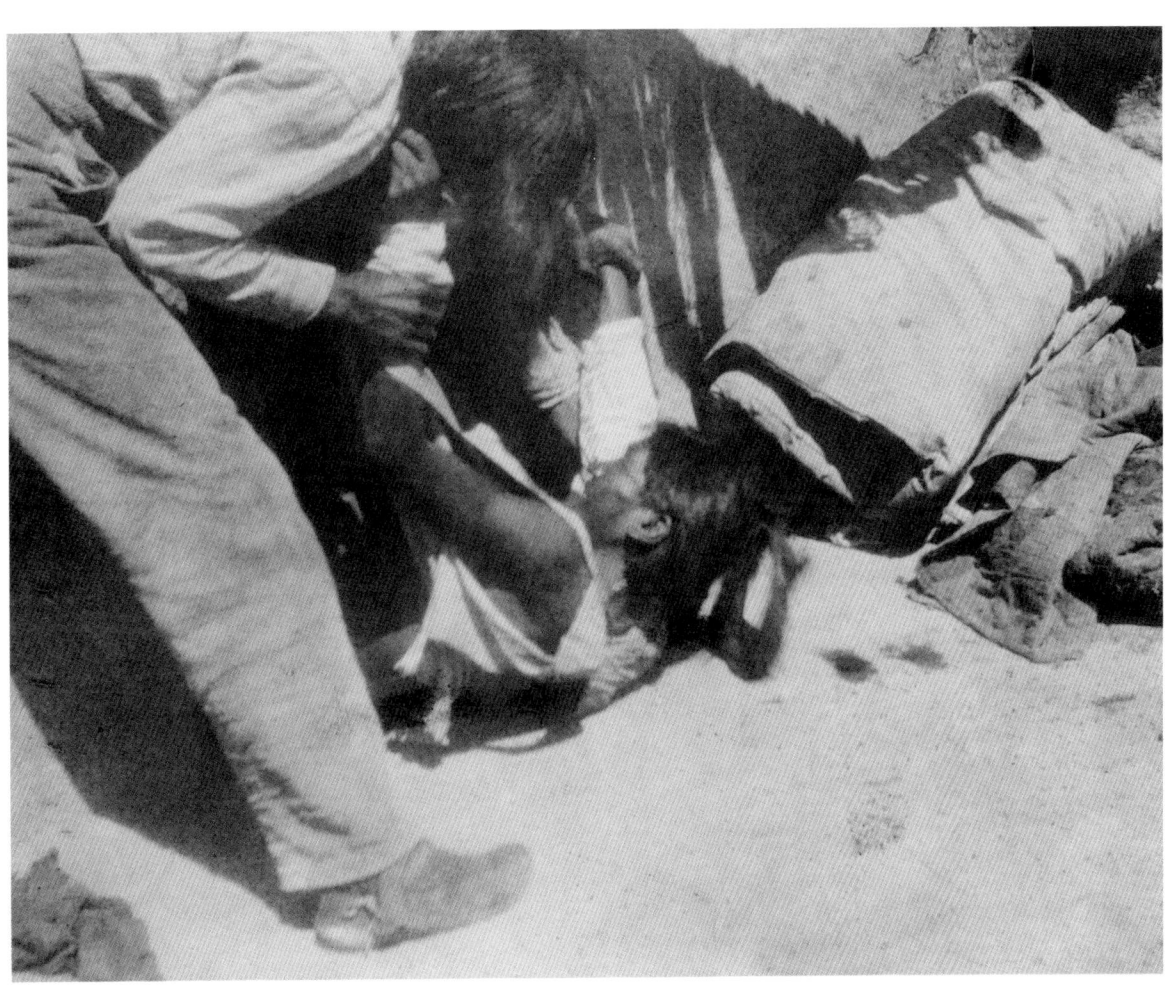

47. ORAIBI as it would have been seen by Father Garces as he entered the morning of July 4, 1776.

"*Descending and turning about I suddenly found myself in sight of the Pueblo. There are two or three tumbledown houses in front of the entrance thereof, and there is to be seen neither any door nor window. The street which is entered is quite wide, and runs straight from east to west, or from west to east, to the exit from the pueblo, and I believe it to be the only one there is. On one side and the other of this are other cross-streets of the same width, forming perfect squares. I saw also two small open places. The surface is not level, but firm. The pueblo is situated with the lower part toward the east, so that only the streets which run from north to south are level. The houses are of heights some greater, others lesser; according to what I found they have this arrangement: From the ground of the street there rises a wall as it were of a vara and a half, at which height is the courtyard, which is mounted by means of a wooden ladder that may be taken away when they wish.*"

ON THE TRAIL OF A SPANISH PIONEER,
THE DIARY AND ITINERARY OF FRANCISCO GARCES

Fr. Francisco Garces (1776)
Edited by Elliott Coues (1900)

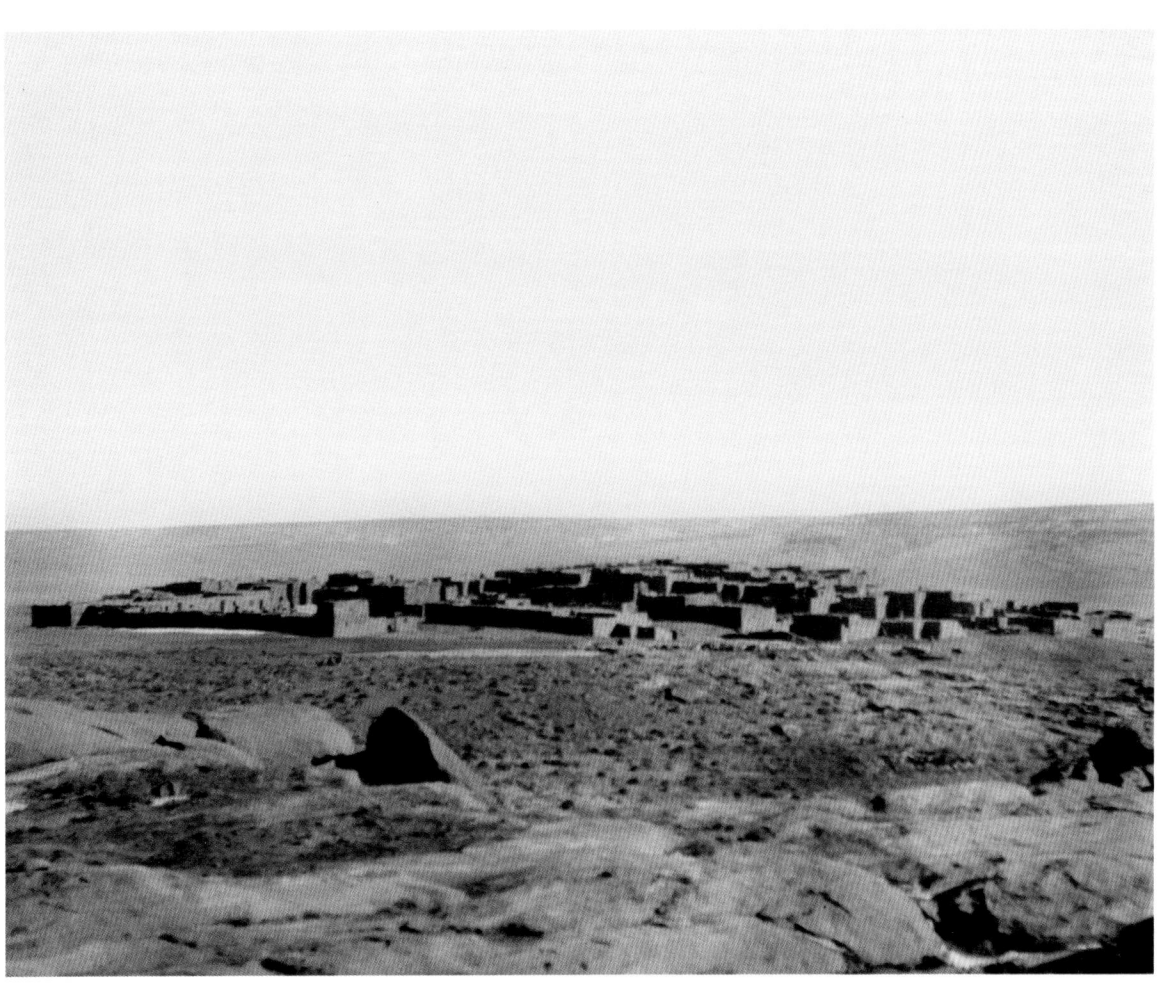

48. THE SNAKE MEN GATHER for their hunt around the Snake kiva.

"On Saturday morning for the first time, a majority of the Tcu'awypkiyas assembled in the Wikwalovi Kiva and prepared for the hunt. They brought with them planting-sticks and hoes, which were laid on the raised hatchway of the kiva while their owners descended to the chamber to prepare for the hunt.

"Each hunter rubbed his body all over with red iron oxide...Besides his hoe or planting stick each priest carried in his hand a little red buckskin bag with fringe at each lower corner and a handle of the same material. It was said to contain sacred meal with which to sprinkle the snakes when they were captured. Each priest also had his snake whip in his hand, and a canvas bag in which to carry the reptiles he might capture."

THE SNAKE CEREMONIALS AT WALPI
Jesse Walter Fewkes, et al. (1894)

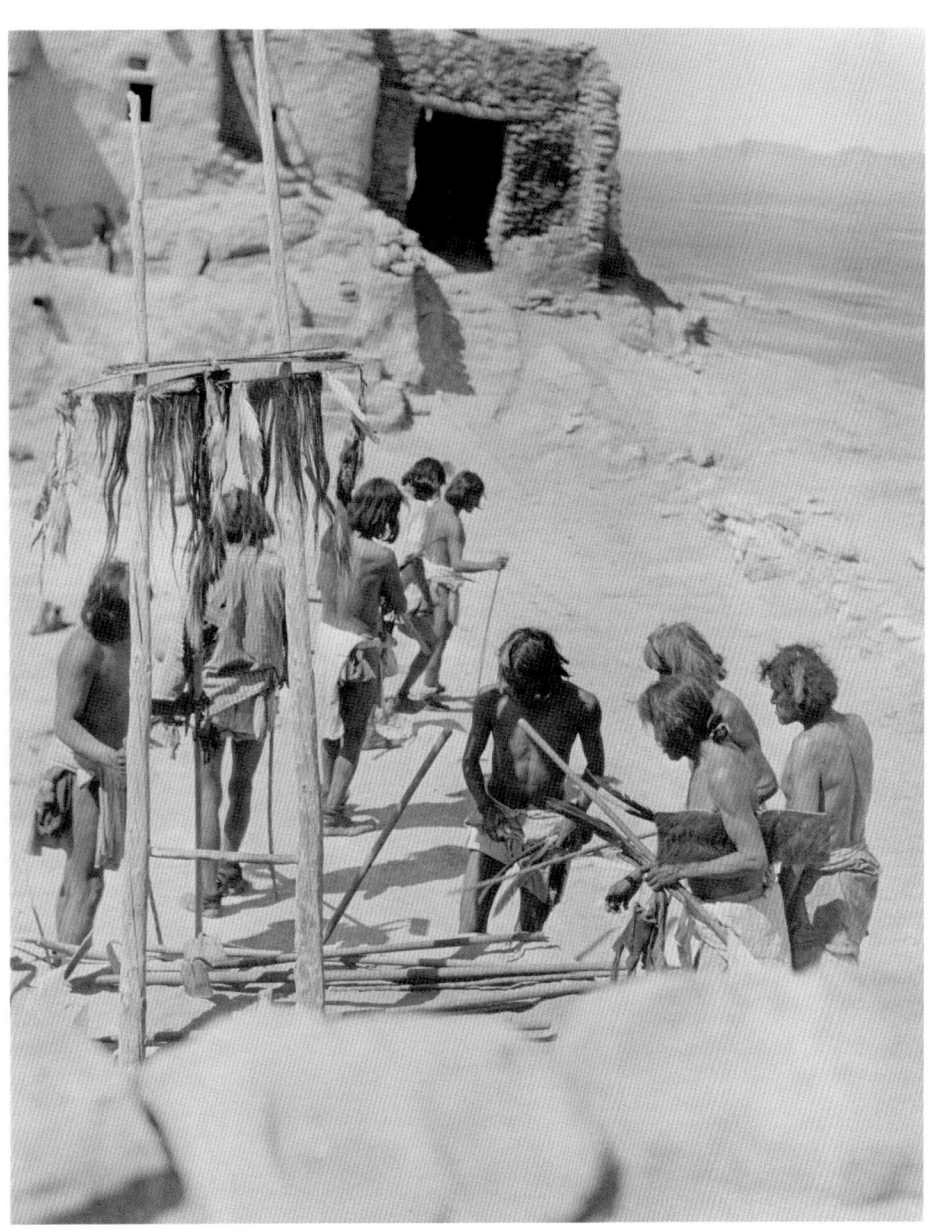

49. A LINE OF SNAKE SOCIETY MEN DESCEND First Mesa on their way out to the valley to gather snakes for the approaching Snake ceremony.

"The Snake men are going out to hunt. After breakfast they go out in a line. After they go down to the foot of the mesa, they go two by two. People have to keep away from the hunters. If anybody meets these Snake hunters, he has to go with them. They have to give him a snake to take into the kiva."

A PUEBLO INDIAN JOURNAL 1920-1921,
INTRODUCTION AND NOTES

Crow-Wing from Elsie Clews Parsons (1925)

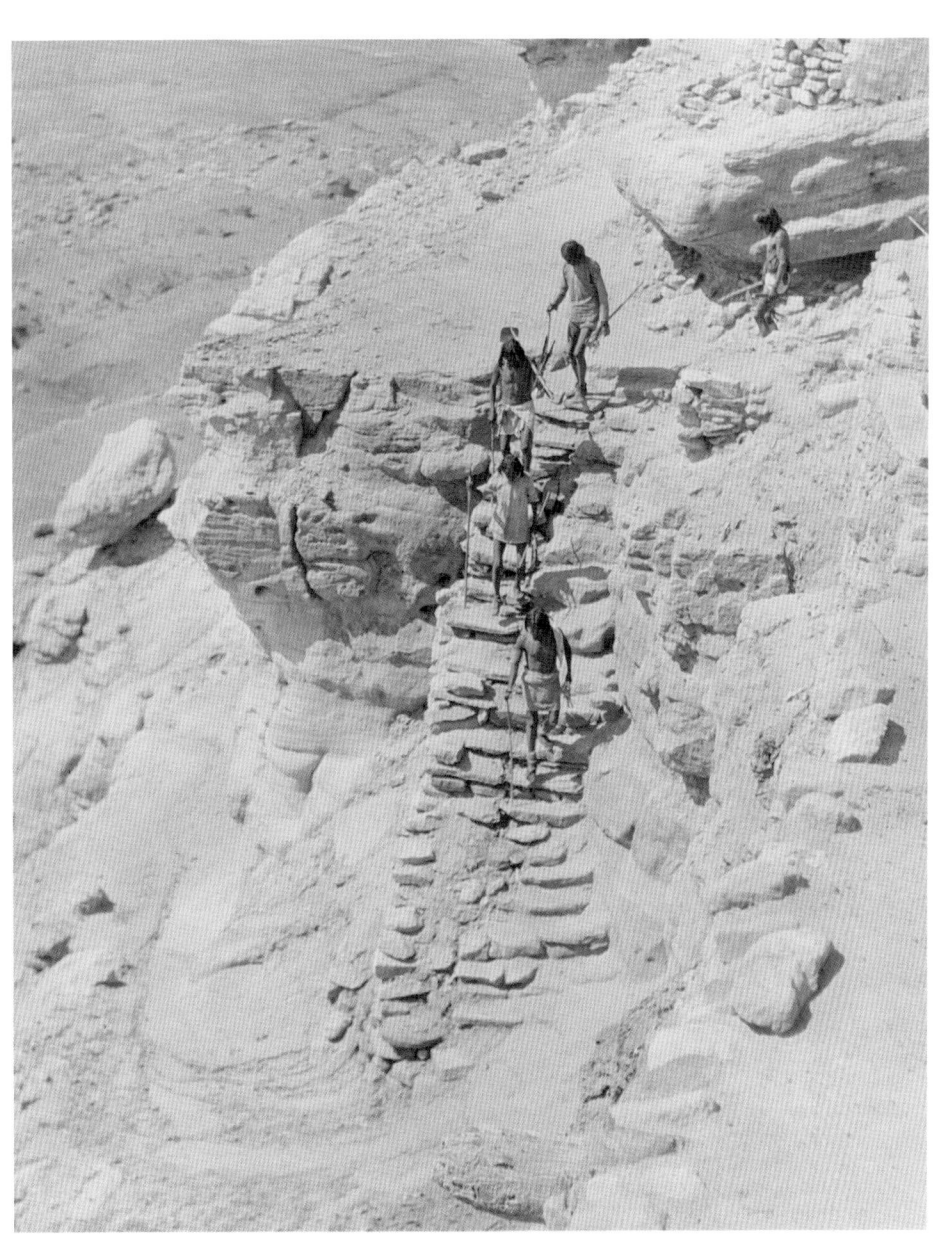

50. A LONG LINE OF BOYS AND GIRLS bearing cornstalks rush up the side of Walpi as onlookers line the cliff edge. Behind them the Kaletaka begins his climb. The rush of the participants in their bright red and white blankets bearing corn stalks is symbolic of the expected harvest following the rains that accompany the Snake Dance.

"As the contestants (of the Snake Race), of whom there were about forty, passed Hon-y, each one touched the crook with the palm of his hand, and sped on his way up the mesa.... Between Hon-yi's position and the foot of the mesa stood a number of girls and boys with corn-stalks in their hands, who also turned and hurried up the mesa sides. The bodies of many of the contestants in the race were painted, and some of them wore flowers in their hair, but none as far could be seen carried pahos."

SNAKE CEREMONIALS AT WALPI
Jesse Walter Fewkes, et. al. (1894)

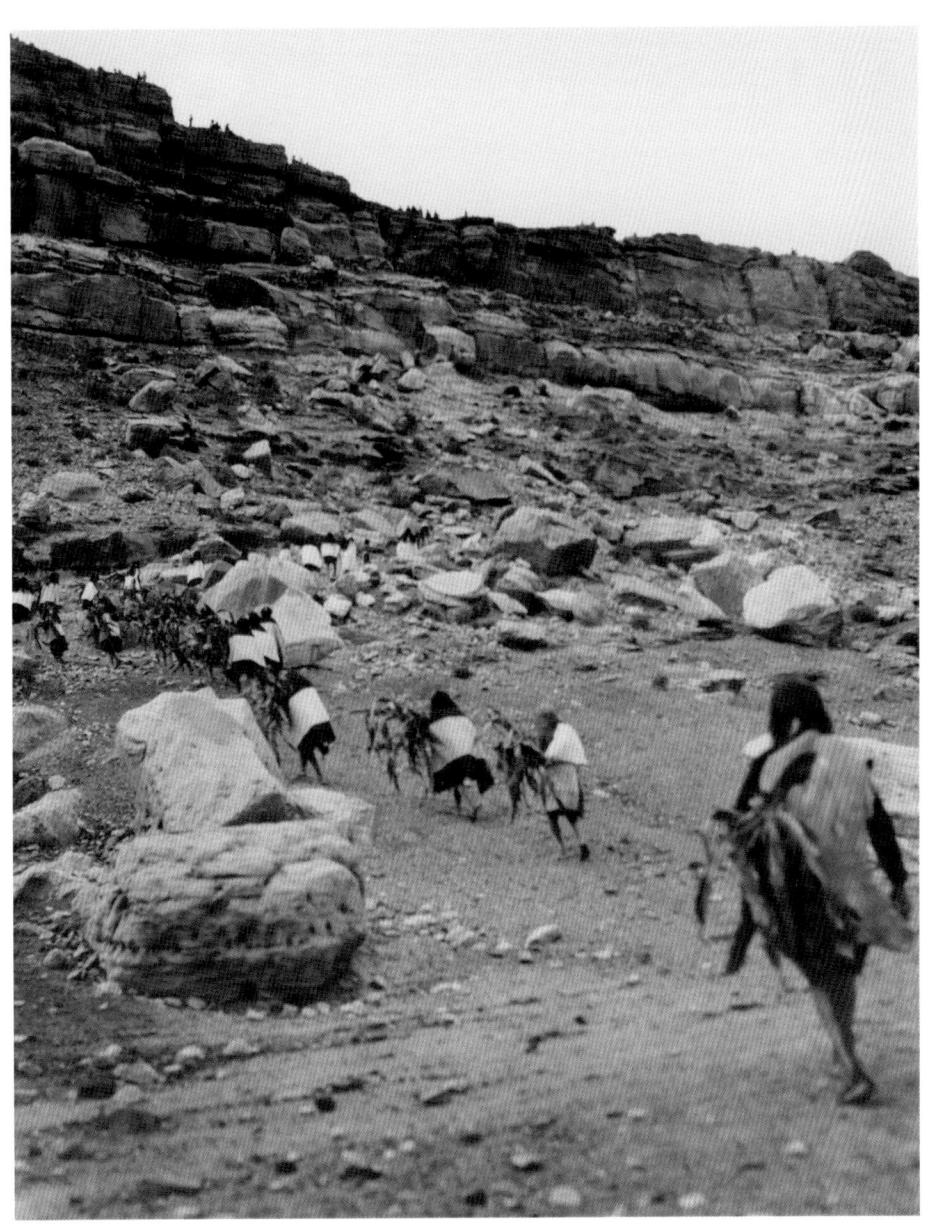

51. THE WINNER OF THE ANTELOPE RACE rushes through the kiskya at Walpi into the north plaza.

"The other event, which occurred outside the kiva on the morning of the eighth day before dawn, was the Antelope foot-race. Seven runners took part, all of whom wore cotton shirts and had rattles tied to their waists. The race was announced long before dawn by the town herald, who called out four times at short intervals. The victor passed through the village just as the Antelopes were finishing their sixteen songs ceremony and dramatization."

THE SNAKE CEREMONIALS AT WALPI
Jesse Walter Fewkes, et al. (1894)

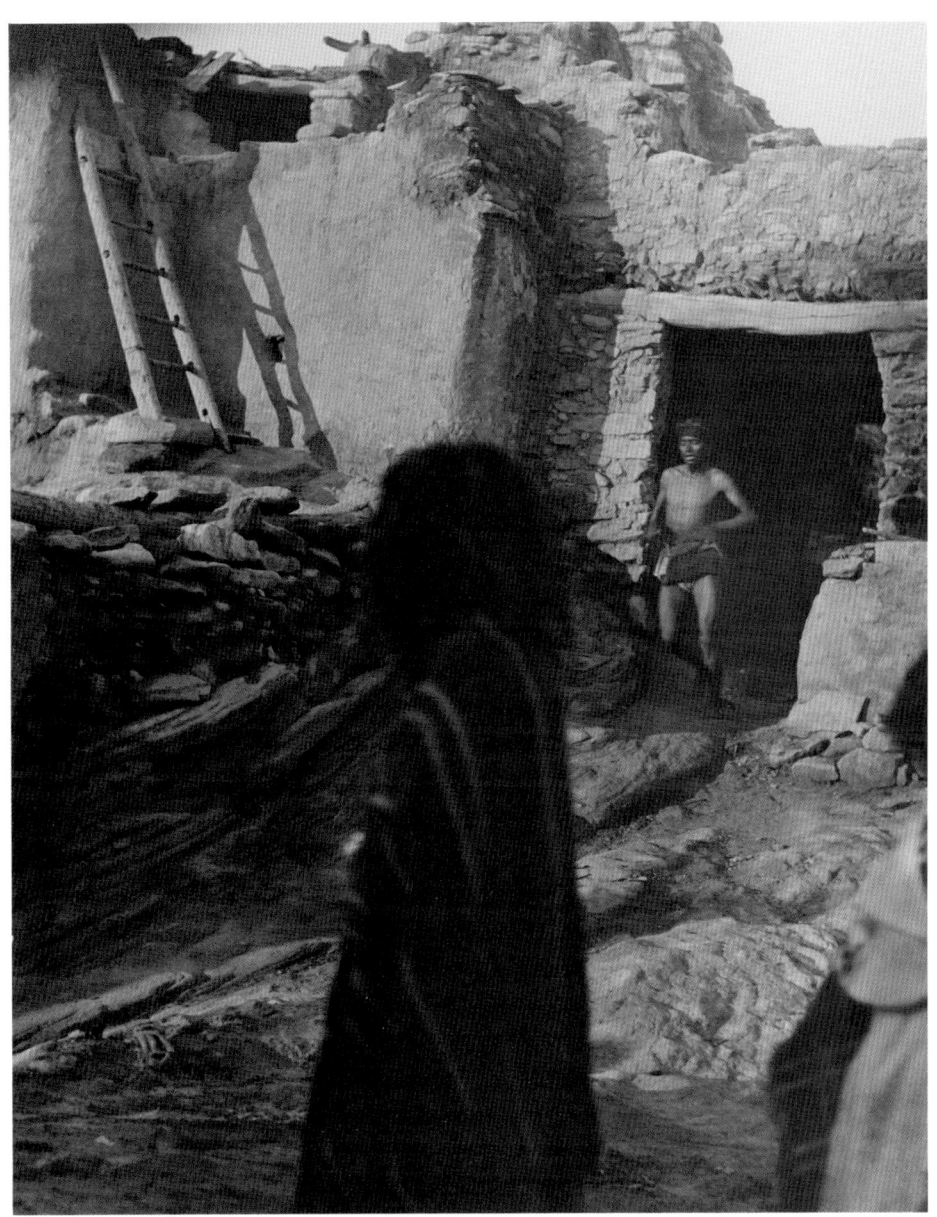

52. SNAKE YOUTH, THE IMPERSONATOR of the mythical Tiyo who began the Snake people, carries the Snake banner or standard across the plaza at Walpi as the Snake Dance begins.

"The ceremonial that follows is referred to as Chü'a Yünya, Snake assemblage, also as Chü'a Yun'ta. It dramatizes the occurrences as seen by Tiyo, the Youth, in the Snake Kiva of the Underworld."

HOPI JOURNAL
Alexander M. Stephen (1936)

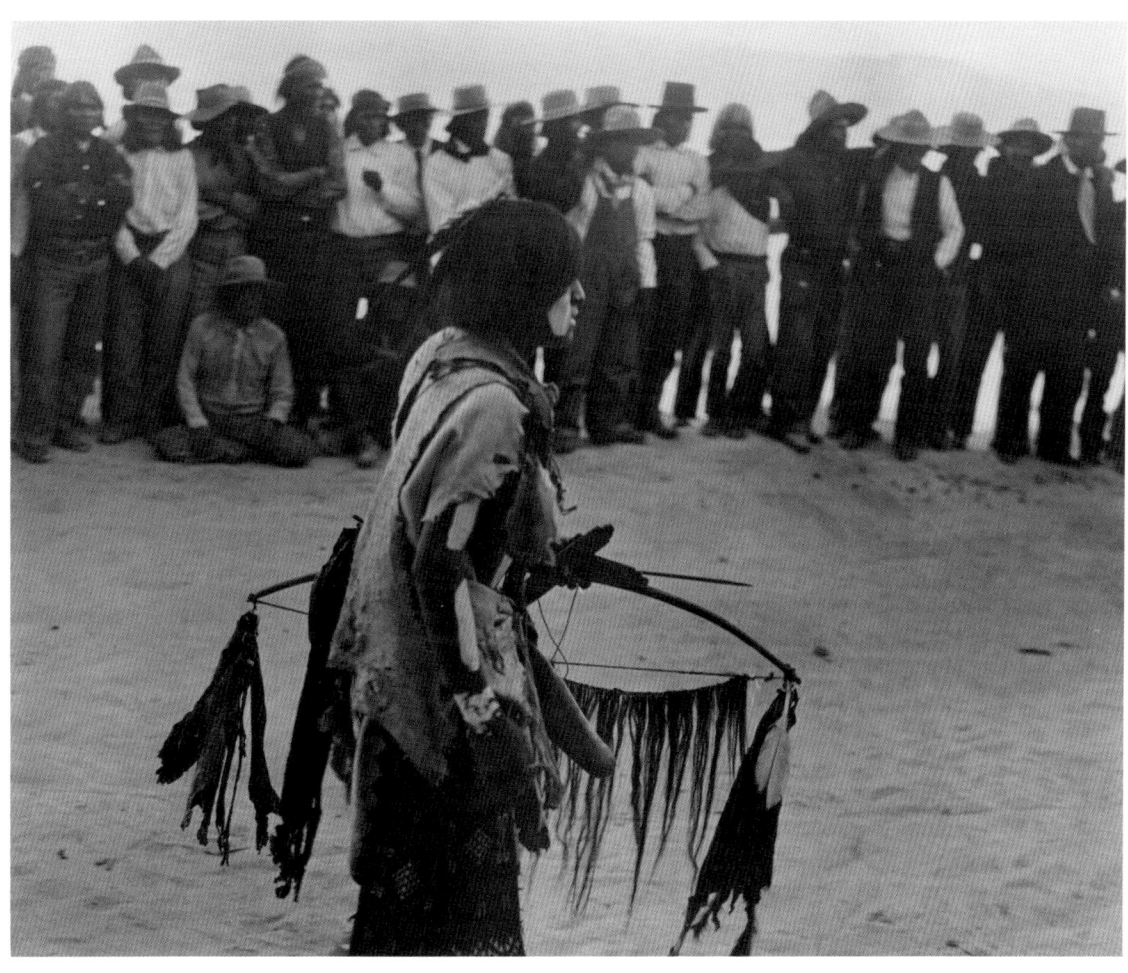

53. SNAKE PRIESTS CIRCLE the plaza as each picks up a snake from the kisi and begins to dance.

"A Snake (priest) stoops down into the kisi and emerges with a snake in his mouth. He holds it gently but firmly between his teeth just below the head. It is a rattlesnake. The flat bird-like head with its unmoving eyes flattened against his cheek, its spangled body dangling like a long thick cord. Immediately another Snake steps up beside him, a little behind, stroking the rattlesnake with his snake whip with intense concentration."

MASKED GODS
Frank Waters (1950)

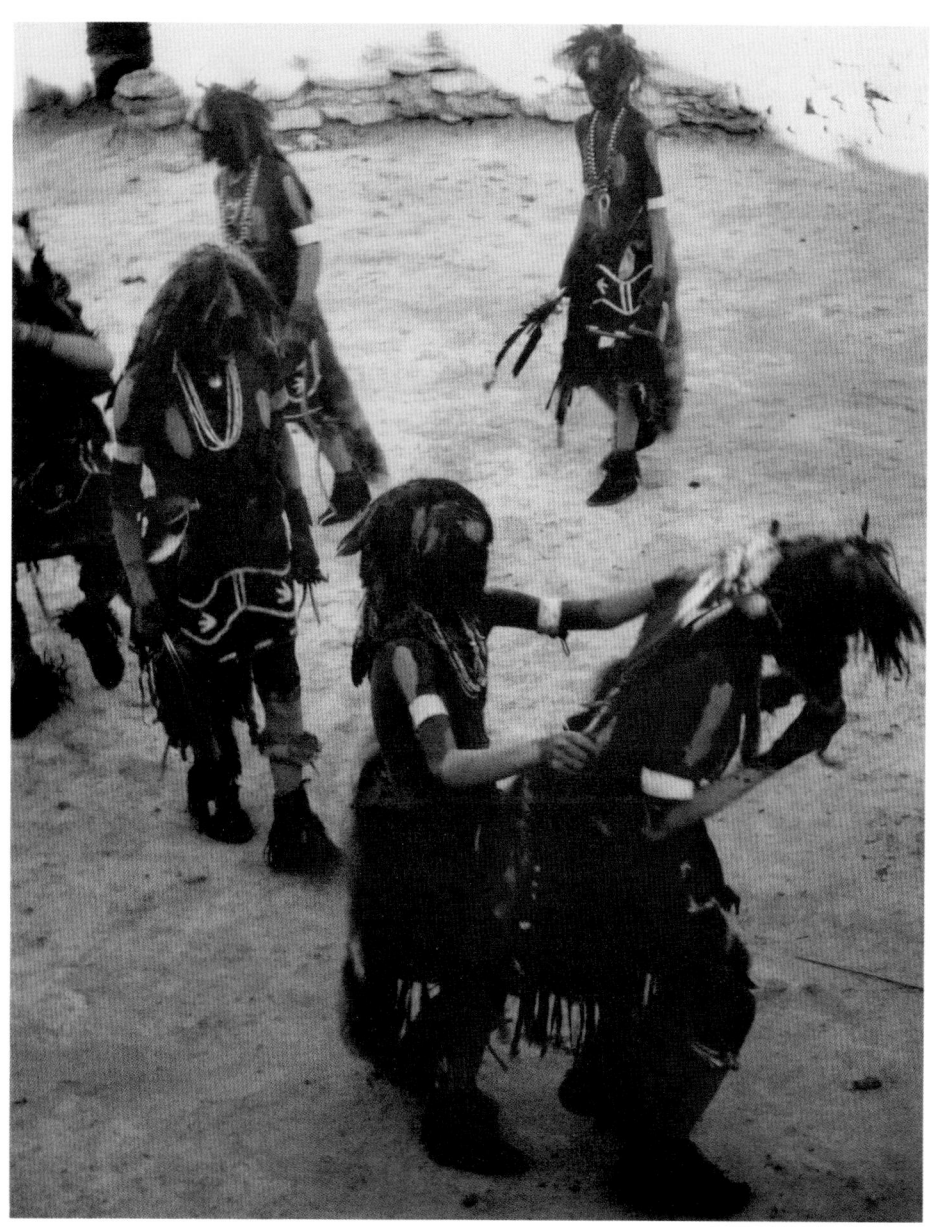

54. THE KALETAKA, OR WARRIOR, who was Mo'mi in Stephen's time, stands on the sand shoulder near Sun spring below Walpi.

"Then Mo'mi with bow and whizzers followed at an interval. All except Mo'mi had a white mantle rolled up and slung over the right shoulder. In these were the last of the prayer-sticks. They passed to the southwest, down the back street, on which is Si'mo's house, around the end of the village and back through the passageway under In'tiwa's house to Chief court and without halt or word down the stair trail and out to Sun Spring."

HOPI JOURNAL
Alexander M. Stephen (1936)

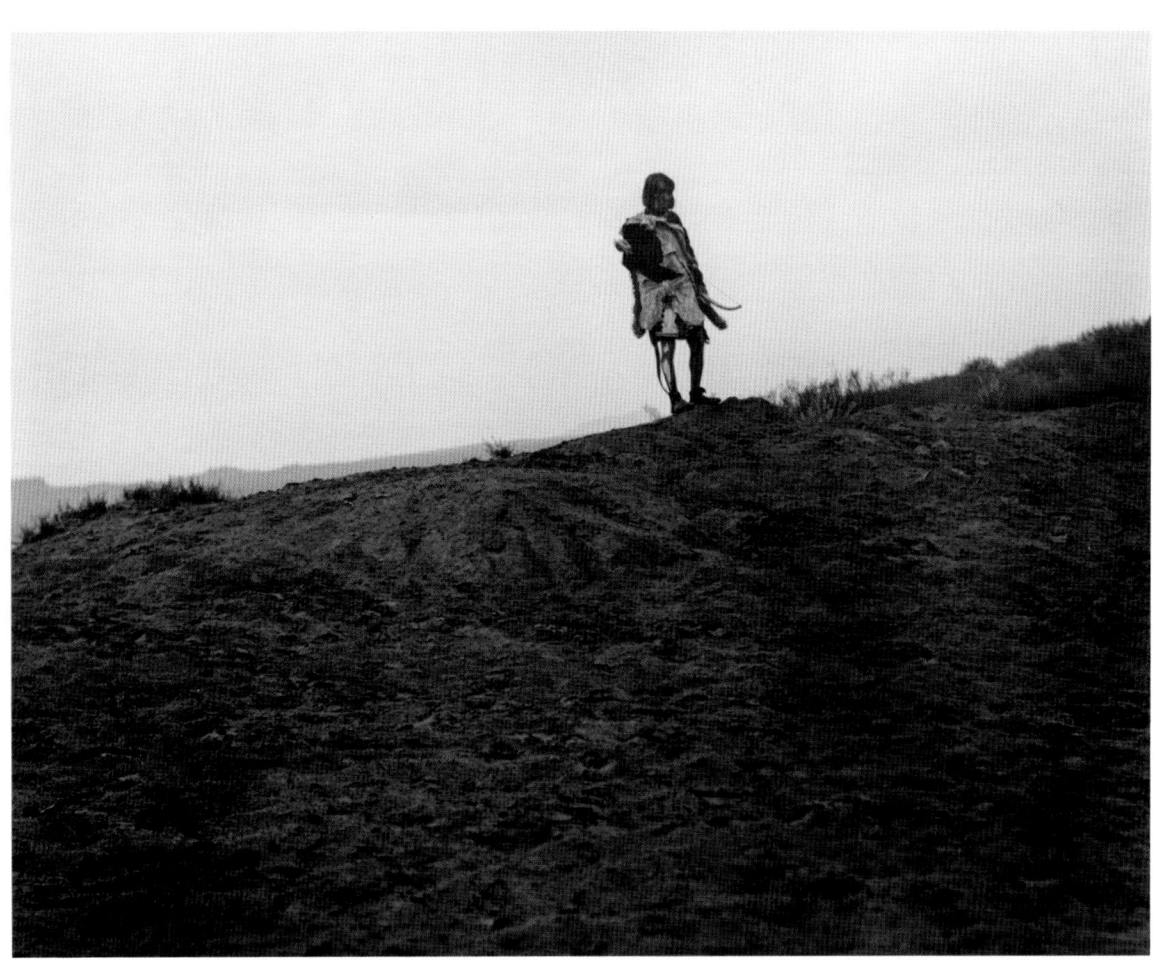

55. ALOSAKTAKA STANDS AWAITING the formation of the procession that will make its way up the sand slope to the trail into Walpi. [This negative was badly damaged *The Editors*]

*"The (Flute) maidens and boy were then told to cast their annulets and cylinder on the cloud sign. They did so, then advanced and picked them up on the point of the prayer-stick...
A losaka, leading, sees that the annulets, etc. are properly cast."*

HOPI JOURNAL
Alexander M. Stephen (1936)

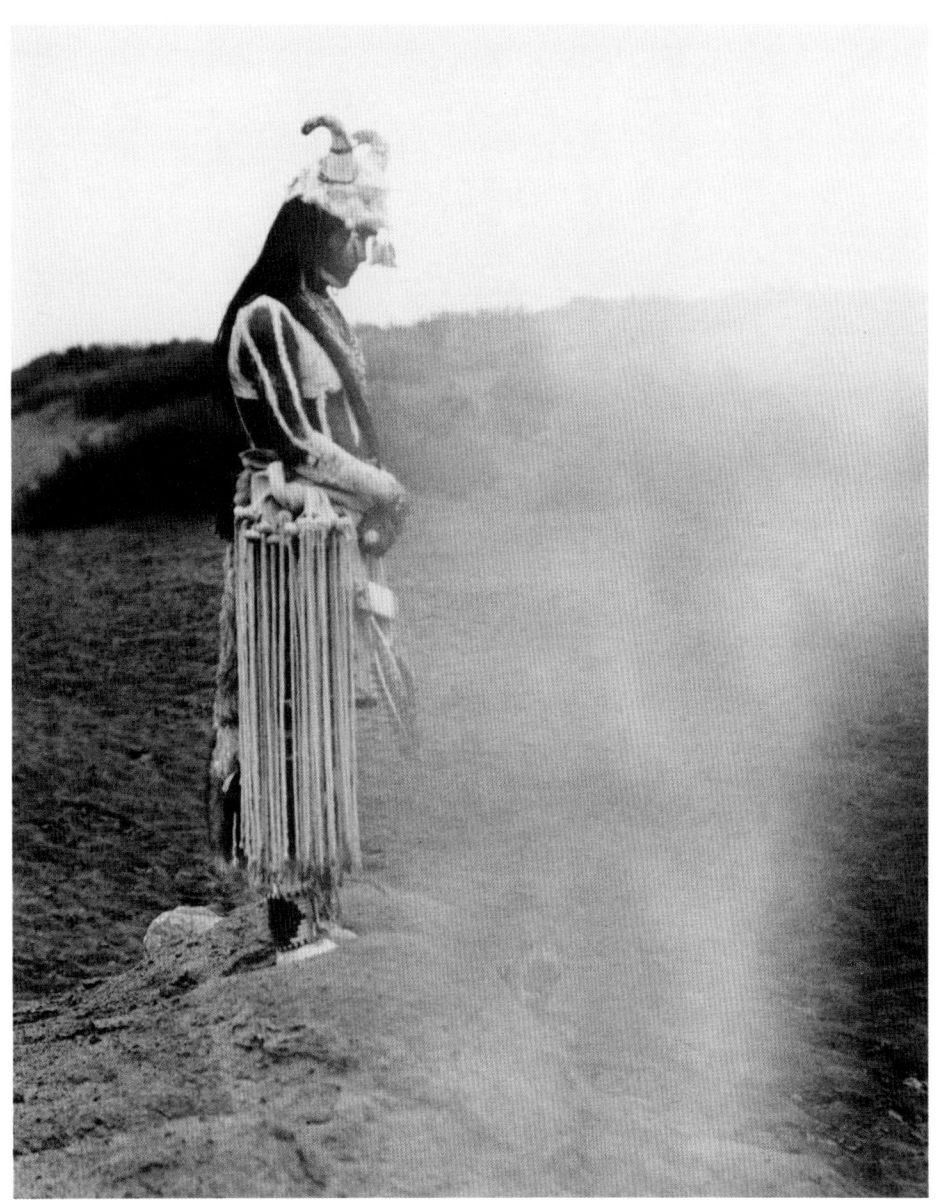

56. MEMBERS OF THE FLUTE SOCIETY sit praying at the edge of Sun Spring below First Mesa. Their day-to-day clothes line the bank behind them.

"There the group sat down on the north side and Si'mo made the four cloud conventions, then he placed several prayer sticks on the oozes on the northwest and southwest sides. They then smoked."

HOPI JOURNAL
Alexander M. Stephen (1936)

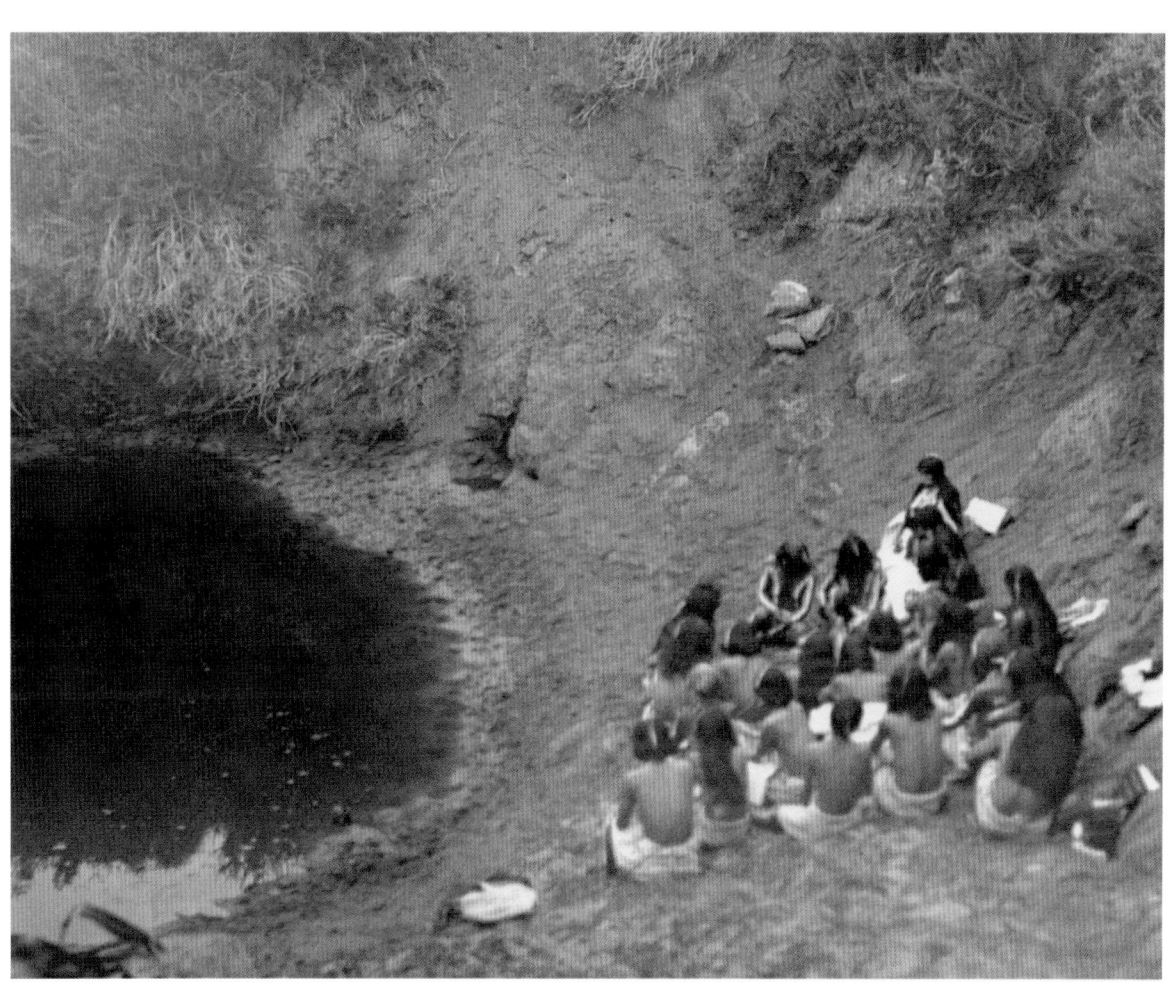

57. THE MAN IS PLAYING YA-HA-HA, holding a bundle or sack with something of value in it. The women of all ages may try to catch him and wrest the object away. Often half of the village may be engaged in this festive action following a Snake or Flute dance.

"For four days after the Flute or Snake dance, boys and men tease girls and women by running about the village with prizes of food or other objects of value which may be taken from them by the females who catch them and seize the prizes."

HOPI OF SECOND MESA
Ernest and Pearl Beaglehole (1935)

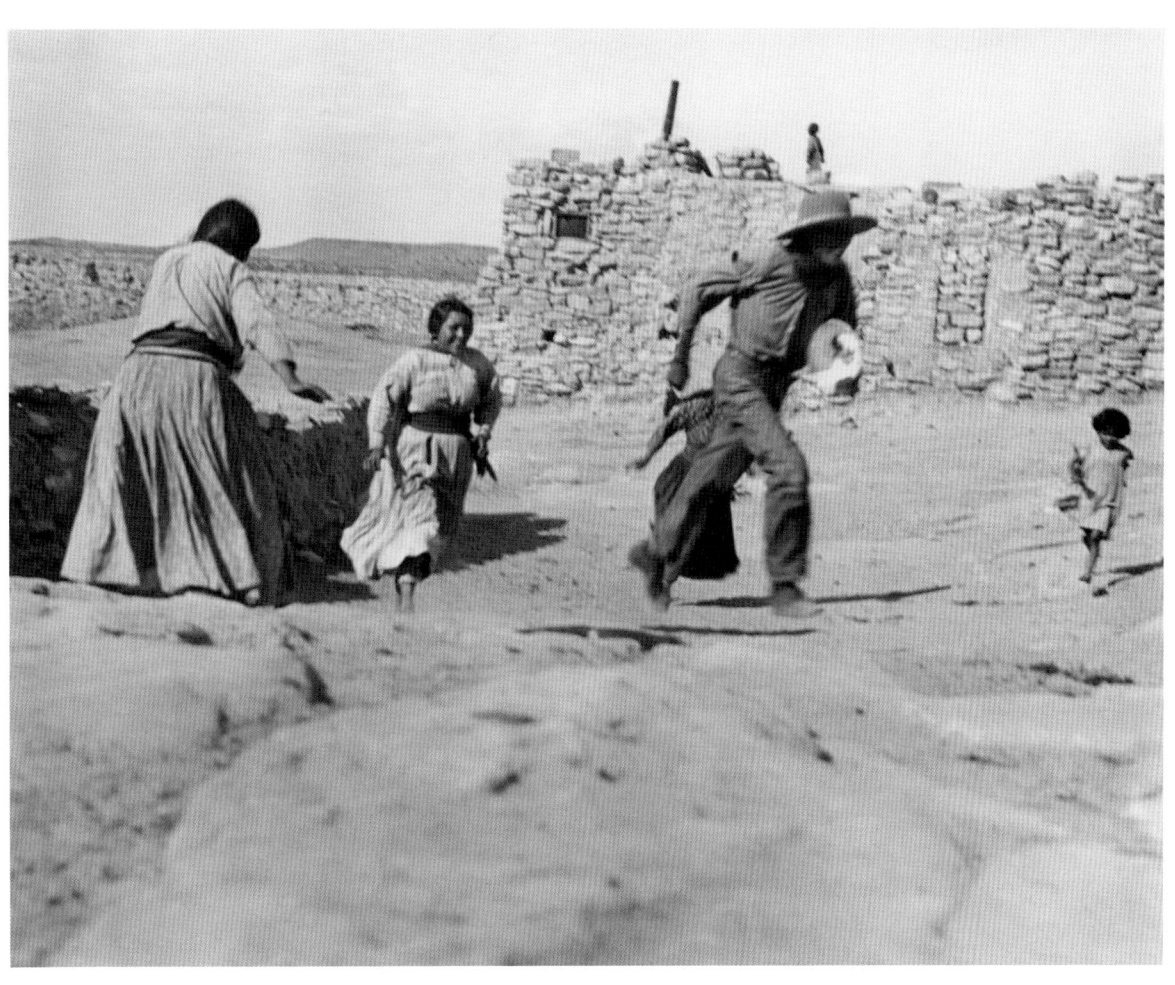

58. As a chorus of men sing in the plaza, Somaikoli is led by the priest Yaya, toward the waiting maiden in the white shawl. Eventually all six Somaikoli will be dancing in the plaza.

"A Tobacco clan man wants to have the dance, so the boys and girls dress up and then they dance. Then the blind kachina come. The men and women bring these blind kachina. The men sing along and the women come and the blind kachina follow them. In the evening, when it is over, the blind kachina go home."

A Pueblo Indian Journal
Crow-Wing from Elsie Clews Parsons (1925)

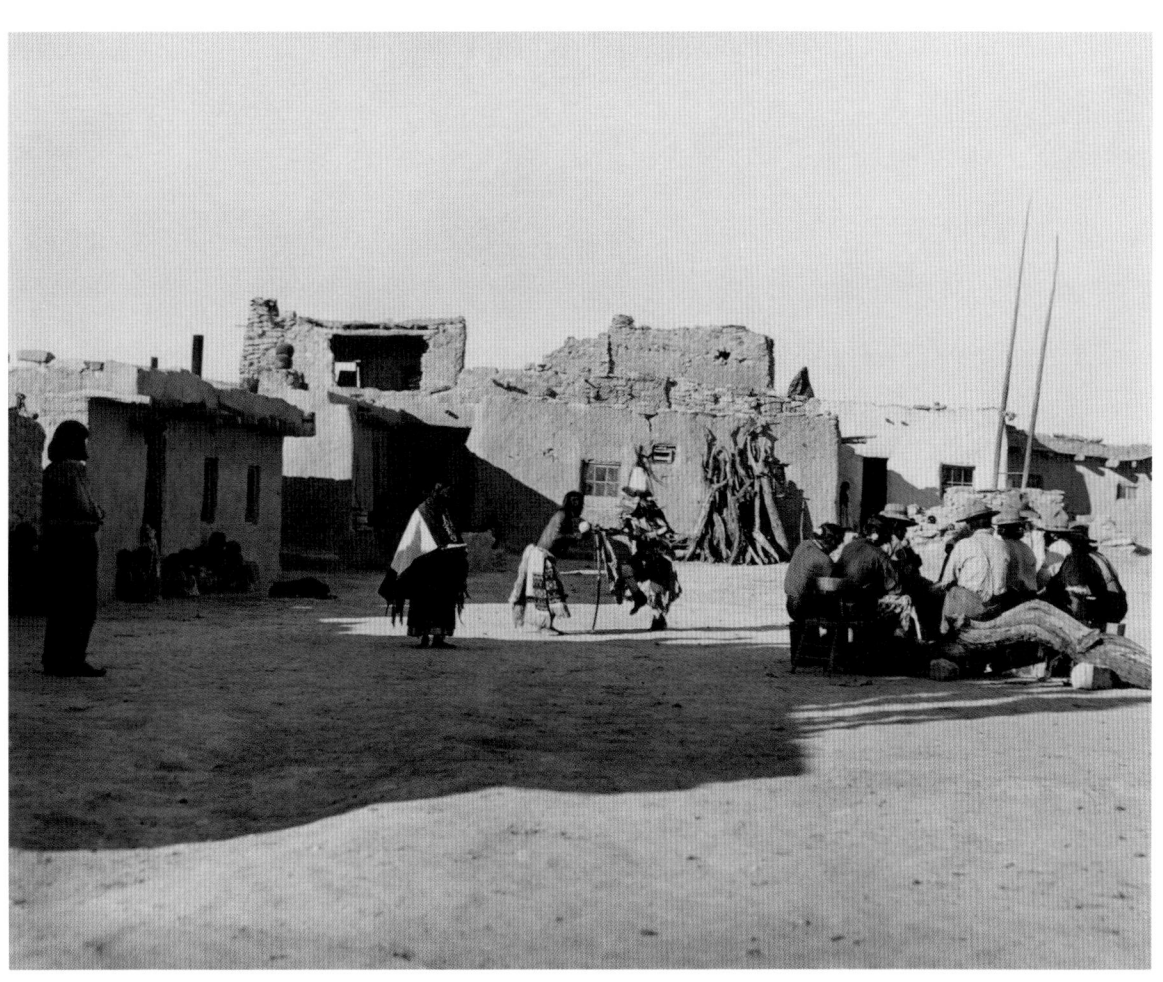

59. SOMAIKOLI, THE BLIND KACHINA, being led by the Yaya priest who accompanies him. The priest holds an unusual rattle in his left hand.

"The Sumaikoli helmet masks of Hano were captured in some Navajo foray and strewn about the base of the mesa. They were gathered by Kalacai and are now kept in pious care in the room near Kalakwai's new house in Hano, where they can be seen hanging to the wall."

HOPI KATCINAS DRAWN BY NATIVE ARTISTS
Jesse Walter Fewkes (1903)

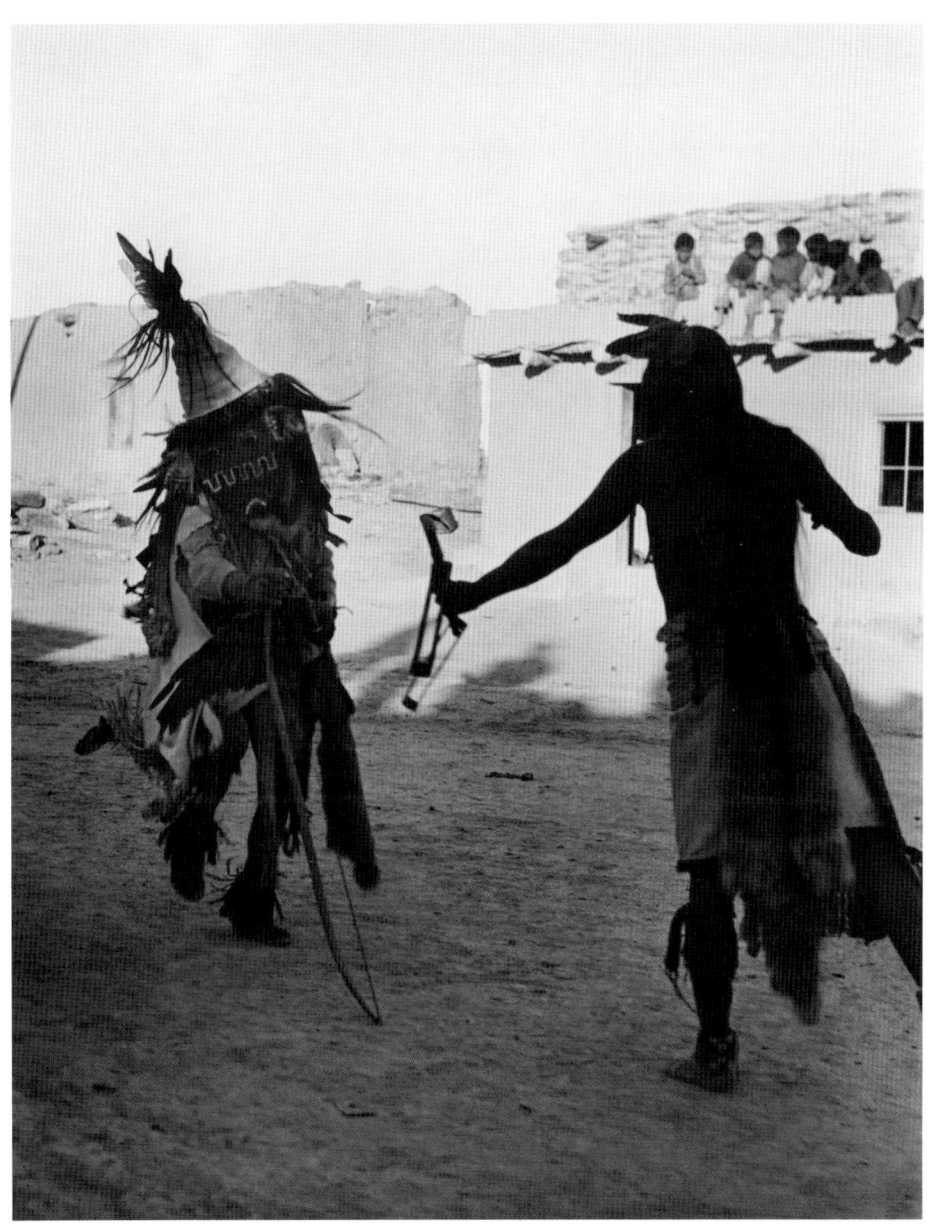

60. TWO SETS OF PALHIK'MANA with their male counterpart, the Palhik'taka, dance in the plaza at Walpi.

"Before them danced two pairs of maids, all costumed about alike, hair hanging loose down the back, the large, gaudily painted carved wood headdress vertically on head; faces rubbed with house meal; string of turquoise beads at each ear lobe; necklaces; white embroidered blanket girt with the big belt and draped as usual; two eagle tail feathers in each hand, held by the quill about vertically; feet and hands yellow. The dance is sort of chasse, gesturing rather gracefully with both hands, and is called pa'lu or pa'lihi'ktipko."

HOPI JOURNAL
Alexander M. Stephen (1936)

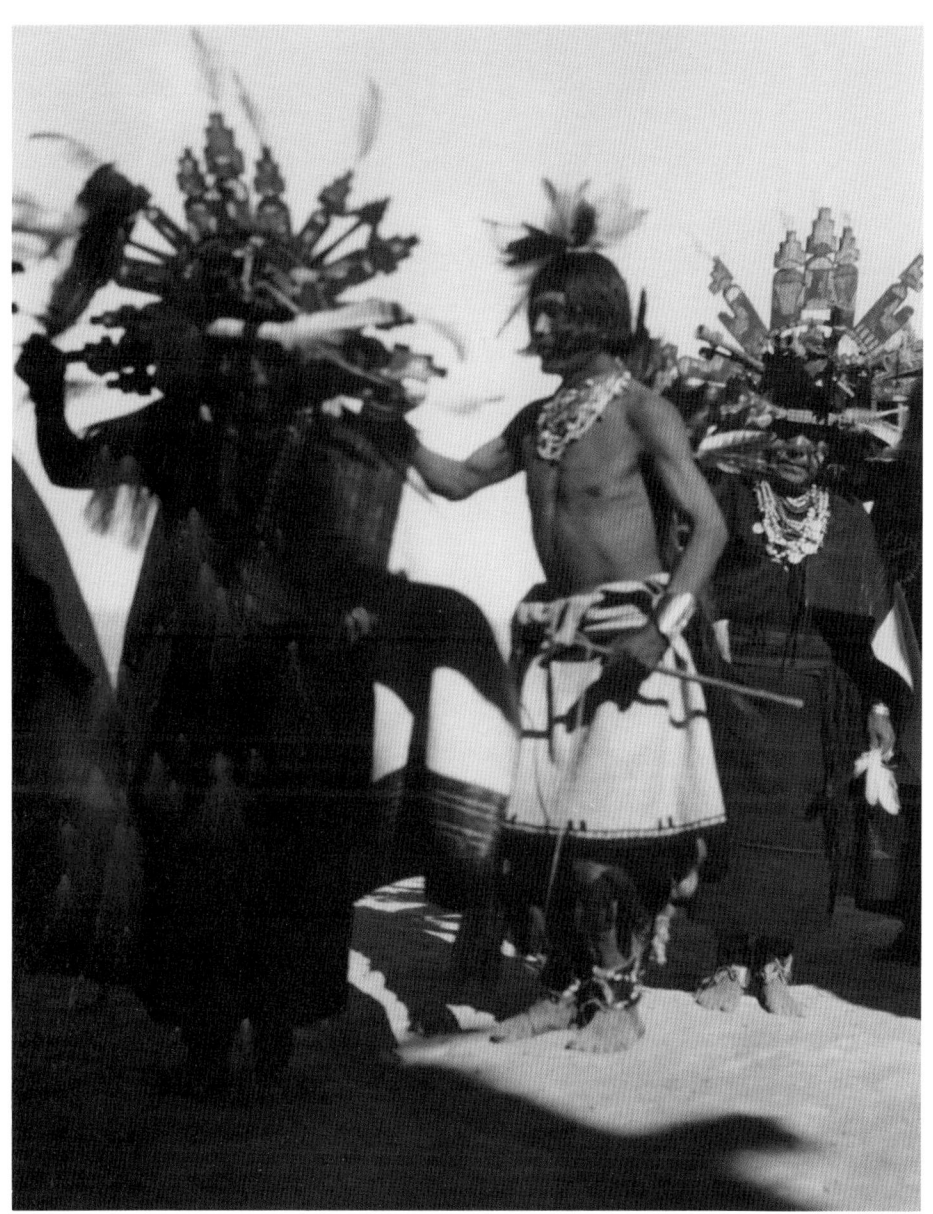

61. Lakone women emerge from the Chivato Kiva at Walpi and prepare to line up for their procession to the plaza.

"The women first left the kiva and went to form a curved line at the Rock [In the plaza at Walpi]."

Hopi Journal
Alexander M. Stephen (1936)

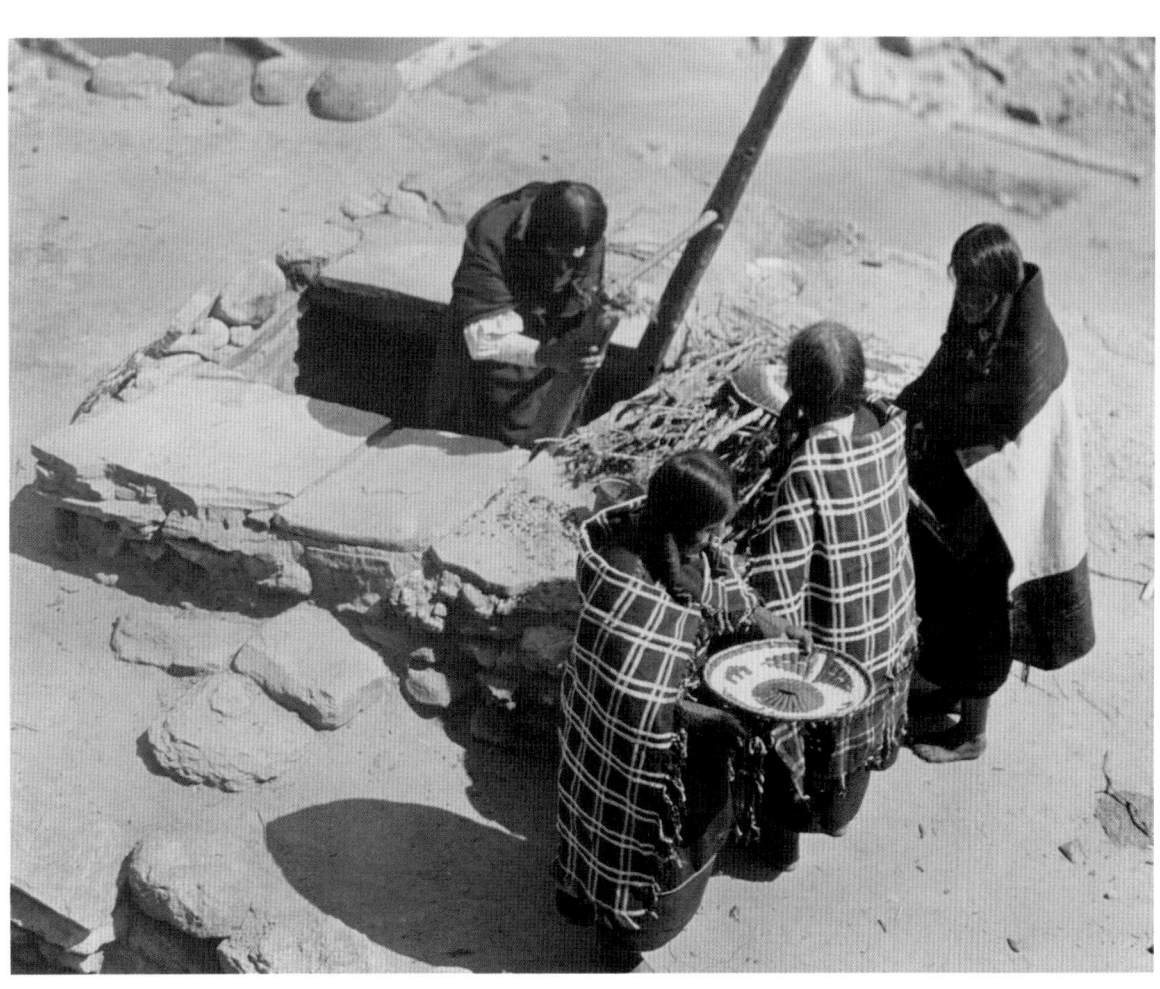

62. THE CEREMONIAL PROCESSION of the two Lakone Manas is assisted by Lakone Taka from the kiva to the plaza where they will bring items to be thrown to the men in the audience.

"Pi'chi then led the two maids who advanced, tossing their corn cobs on the ground, till they got within the curve. As they threw the cobs down, Pi'chi picked them up and returned them to their hands."

HOPI JOURNAL
Alexander M. Stephen (1936)

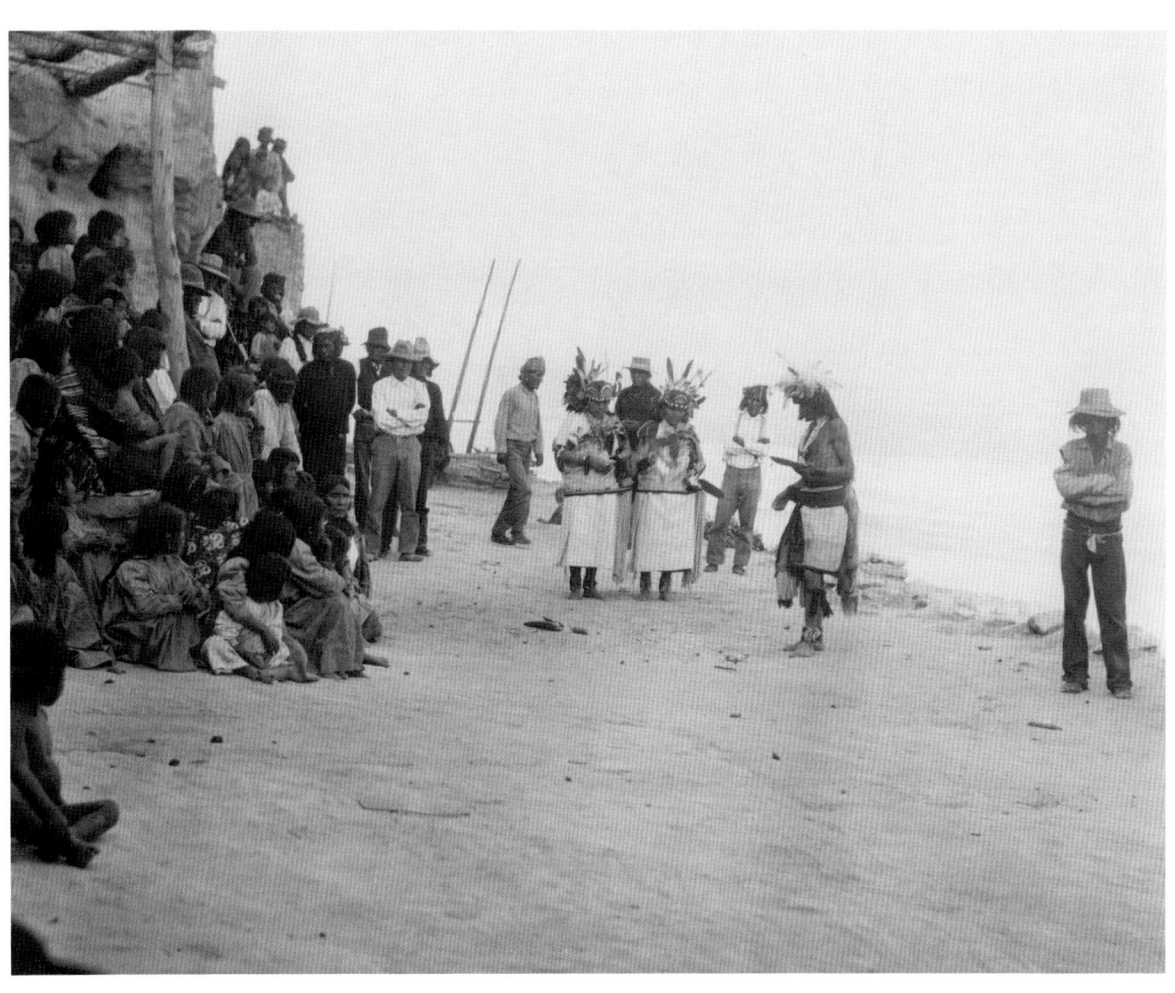

63. MEN STRUGGLE IN THE WALPI PLAZA to retain a basket thrown out by the Lakone Manas. Quite often the item thrown is destroyed in the effort.

"At the fourth change each girl threw the scone (a Hopi bread rather than a scone) she held in her hand as far as she could among the group of men who stood around anxious to seize. After all were gone, they threw among the men the large tray basket which held the bread."

HOPI JOURNAL
Alexander M. Stephen (1936)

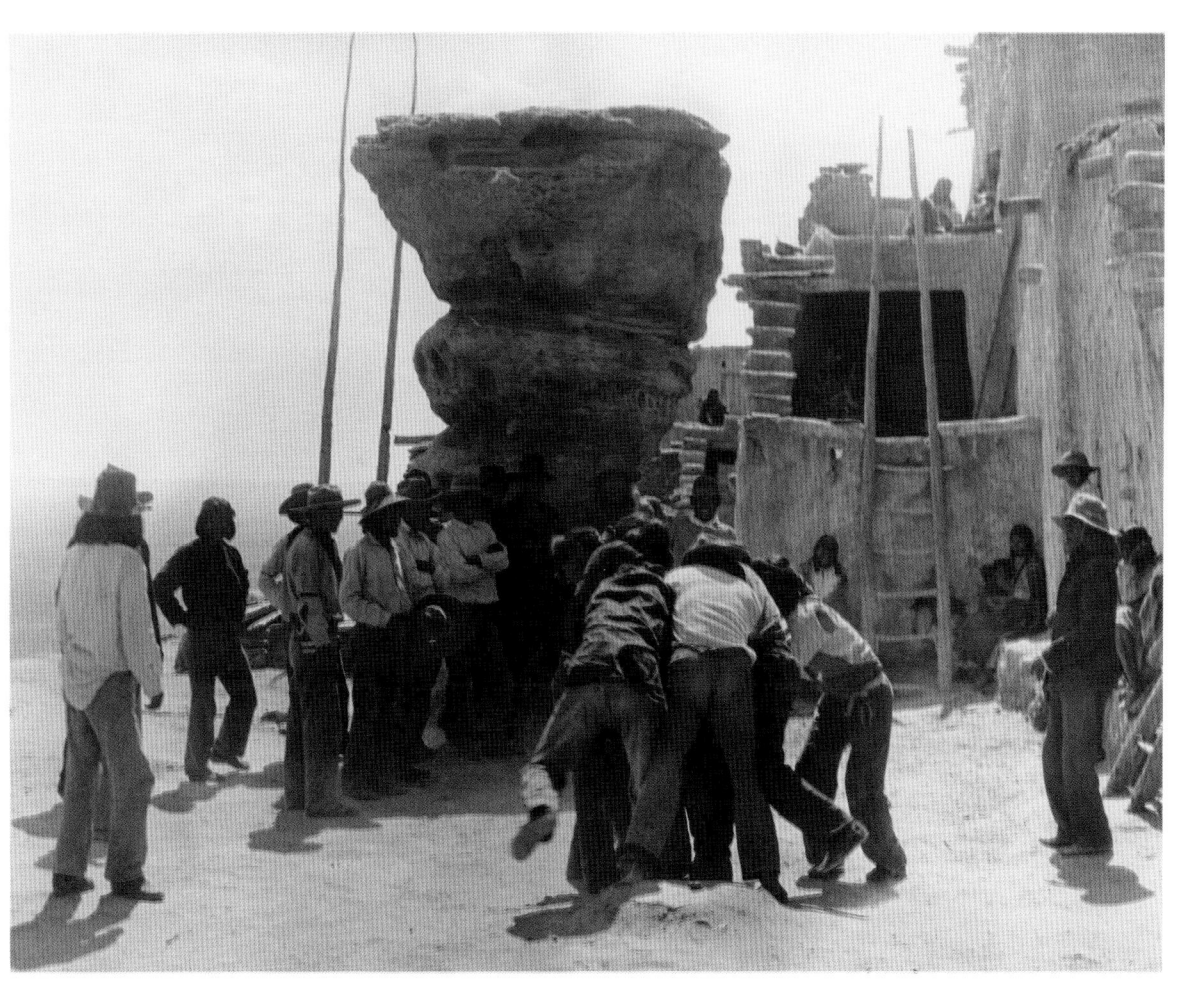

64. THE LAKONE SOCIETY WOMEN perform a basket dance in the plaza at Walpi with one of the two Lakone Manas in the center of the curve.

"On the dance plaza were thirty-five women and girls from all three villages. Women stood in the form of a horseshoe, the broken circle, gap, toward the east. All had a basket in hand which they moved up and down before them while they sang, only a few minutes, not more than five. They then filed off to the Goat Kiva."

HOPI JOURNAL
Alexander M. Stephen (1936)

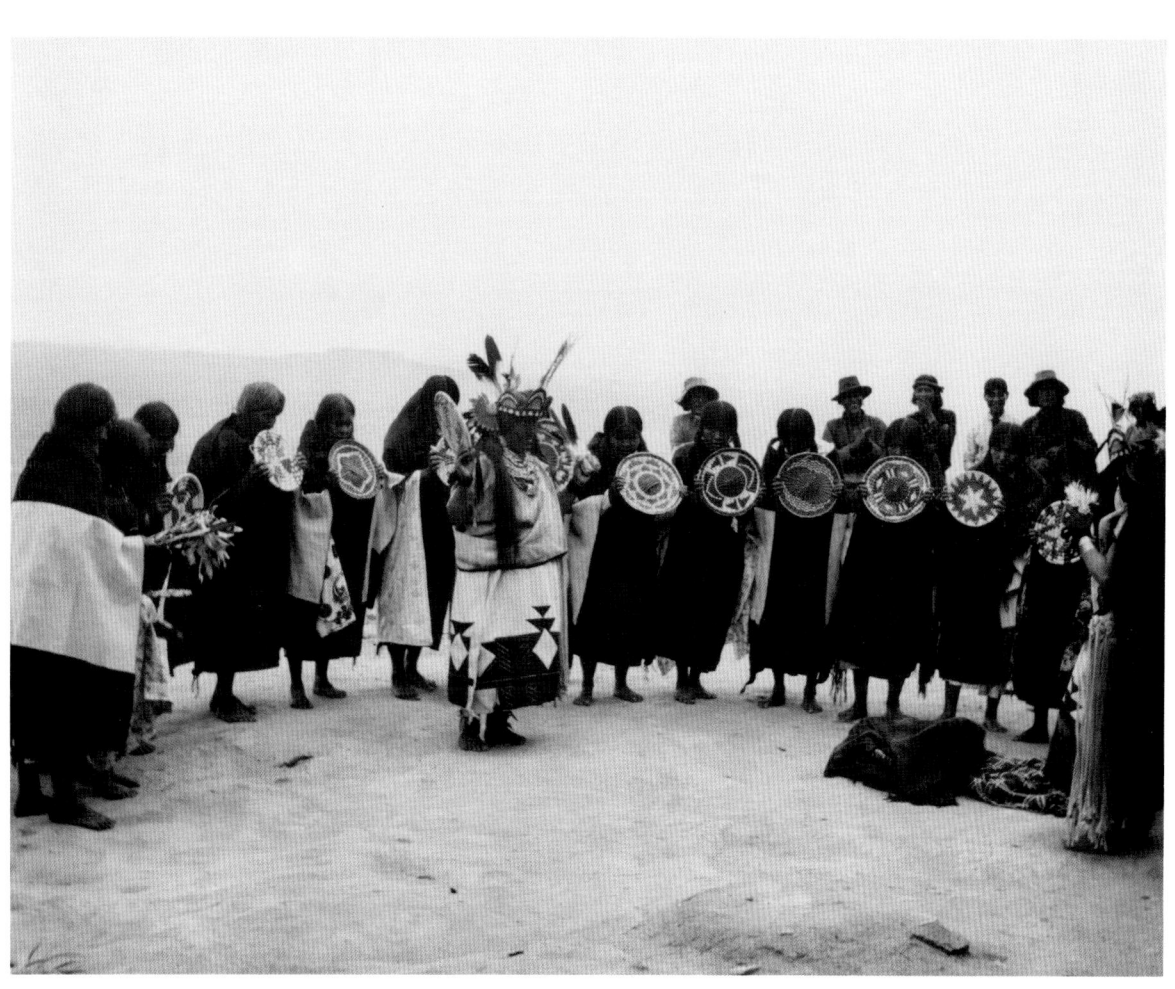

65. MEMBERS OF ALL of the societies cluster around the kiva hatch in the first cold light of morning during the Wuwuchim ceremony.

"It was piercing cold, and the song ceased just at the first streak of dawn, when the Kwa'-kwan-tu returned to the kib-va."

THE NA-AC-NAI-YA:
A TUSAYAN INITIATION CEREMONY

Jesse Walter Fewkes (1892)

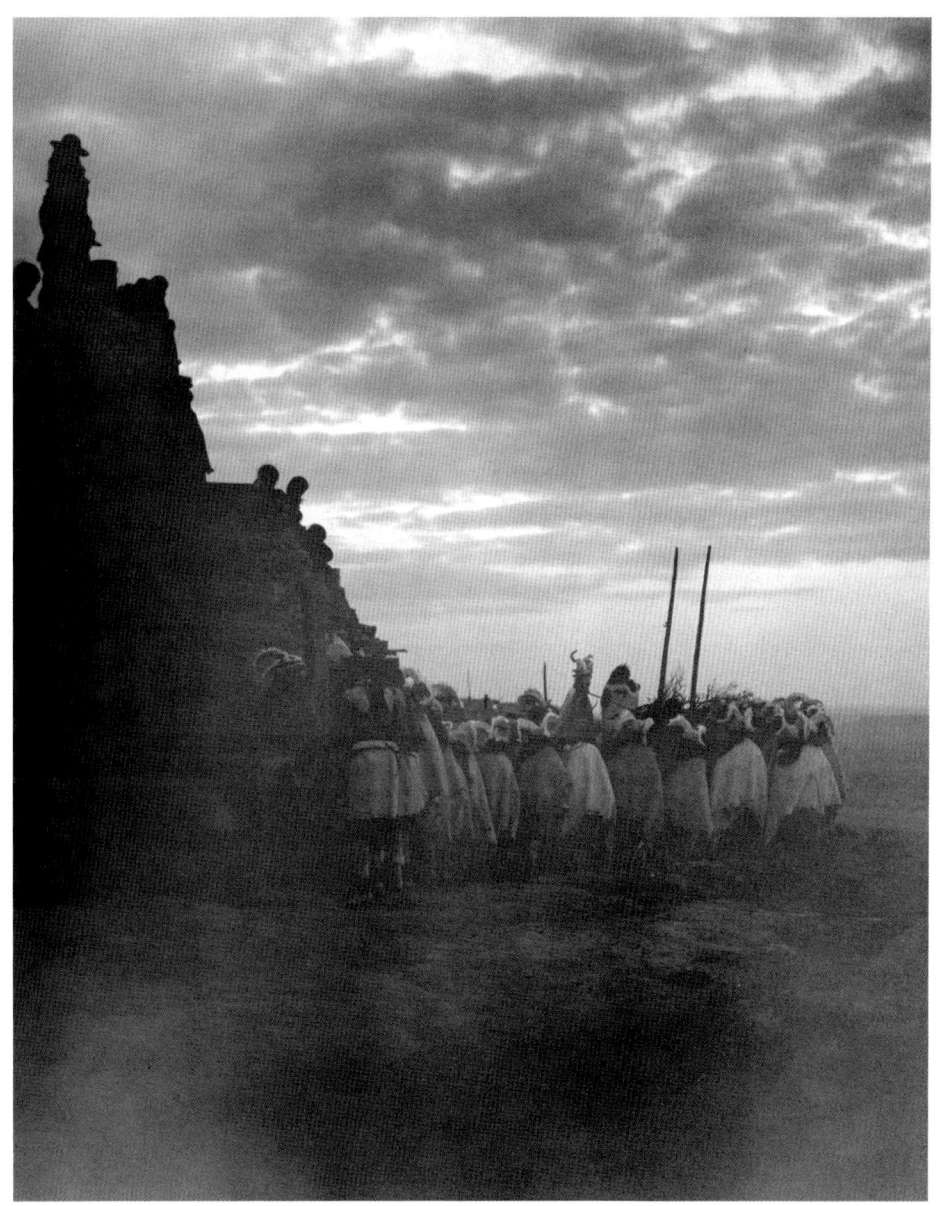

66. MEMBERS OF THE TWO-HORNED PRIESTS' society perform their ritual around the Mong Kiva at the western end of Walpi.

"During one of our sacred ceremonies the One-Horn and Two-Horn societies close all the roads that lead into our villages. They do that so as to clear the spiritual highway which leads from there to the rising sun. This is a road over which they walk to offer their prayers to the Great Spirit. . . . During that special day it must not be broken by someone traveling across it. If it is broken, something unfortunate happens."

THE GREAT RESISTANCE,
A HOPI ANTHROPOLOGY

George Yamada (1957)

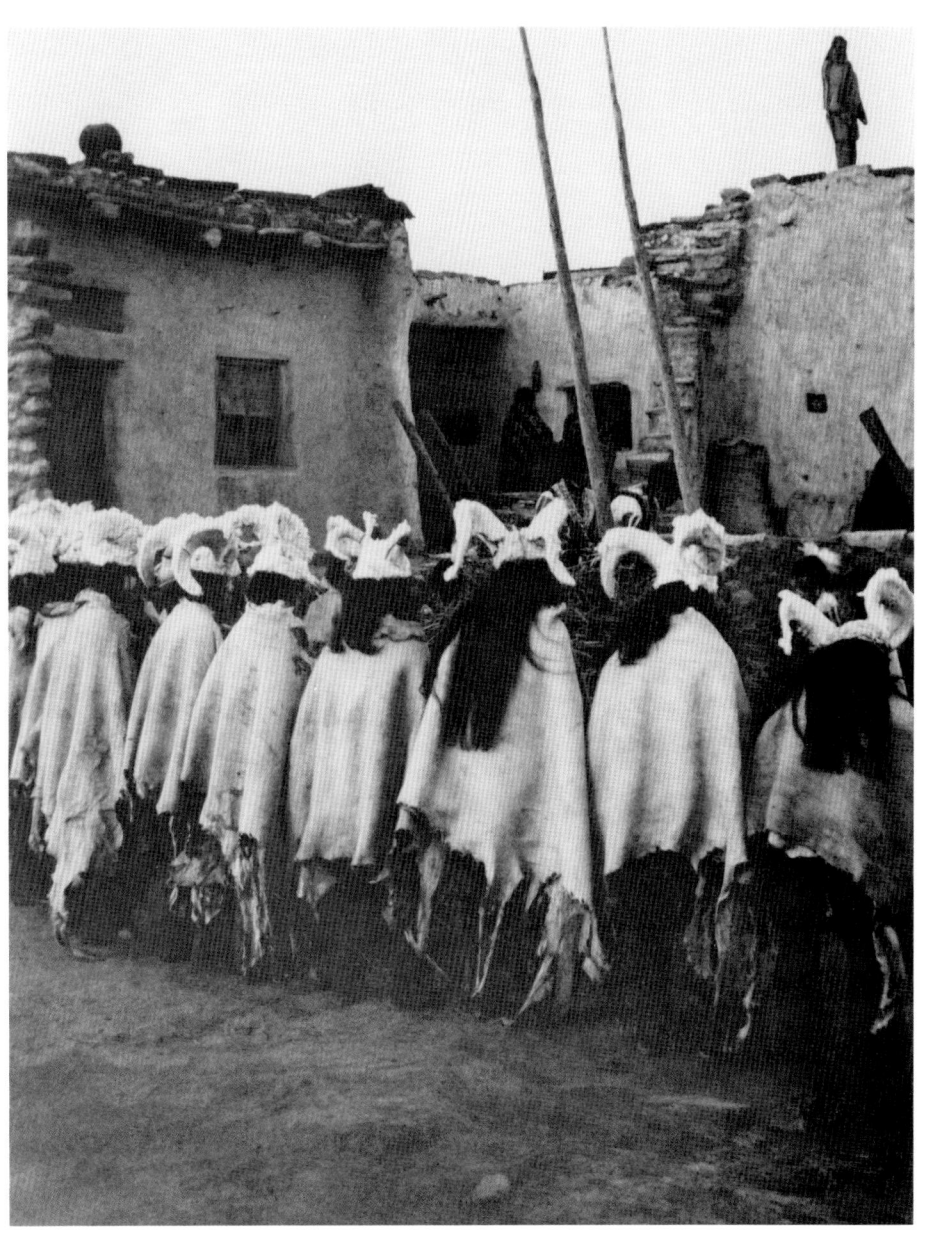

67. DURING THE WUWUCHIM RITES members of the four Hopi societies perform a shuffling procession that passes from one ceremonial point to another. Members of several societies have been captured in this photograph, including two *Aahl* (Two-horned Society) men with their huge curved horns.

"The head-dress worn by the men of Aaltu society represents horns of the mountain sheep, mounted on a cap of basketry. These horns, which are often of huge size, are made of buckskin and painted white. Raw cotton is glued to them, and feathers attached to strings hang down over the face of the wearer."

THE NEW-FIRE CEREMONY AT WALPI
Jesse Walter Fewkes (1900)

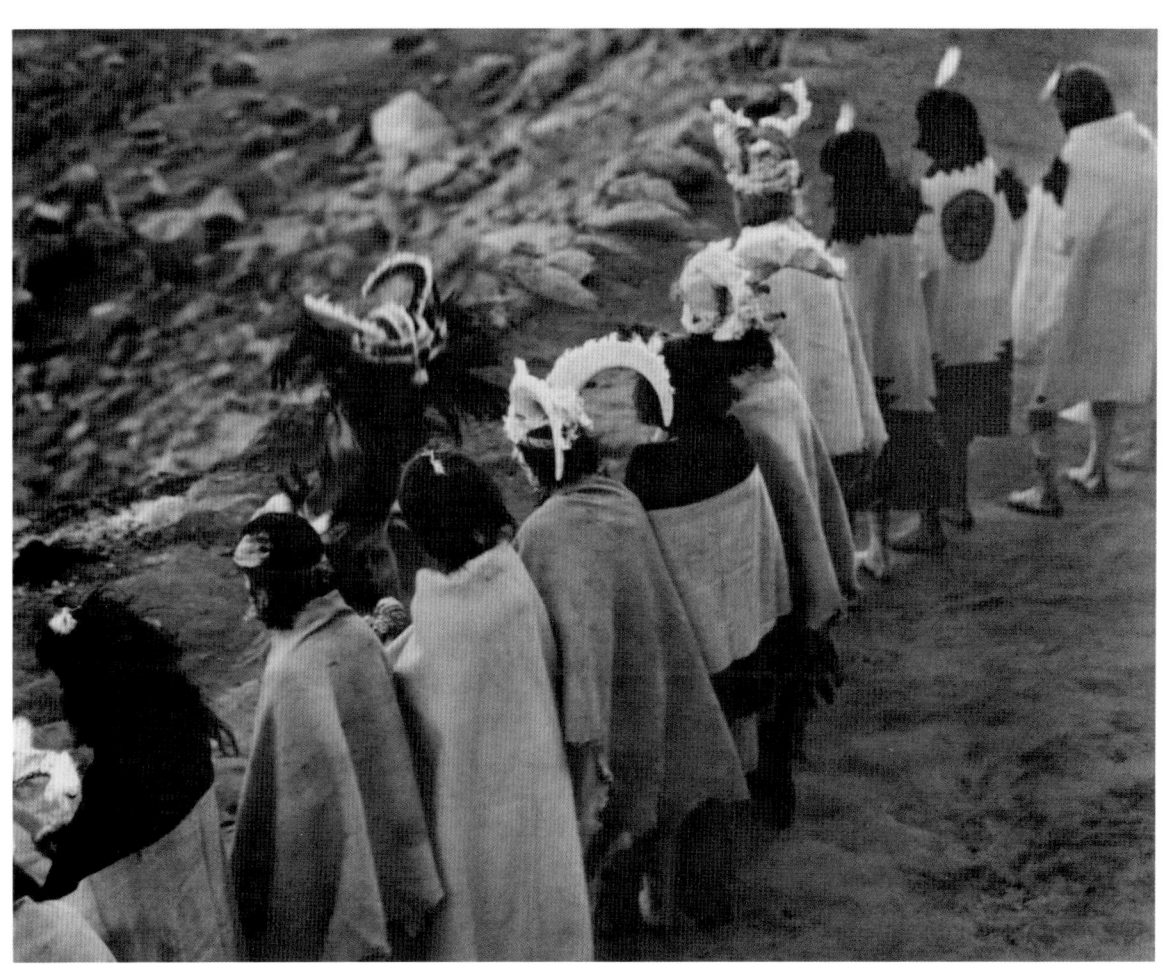

68. IN THIS RARE PHOTOGRAPH, the entire membership of the Two-Horn Society moves in a side-stepping line through the streets of Walpi following their night patrol when deceased ancestors revisit their homes.

"... the deserted streets on the fourth night are patrolled by the Kwan and the Horn men who keep up a fearful din, the Kwans with bells and the Horns with hoofs and tortoise-shell rattles. ... The patrols challenge and club at anything they see, except the proper dead. These patrolmen go back and forth through the village in an anti-sunwise circuit; since the dead are the reverse of the living, the performance must be the opposite of normal behavior ..."

PUEBLO INDIAN RELIGION
Elsie Clews Parsons (1939)

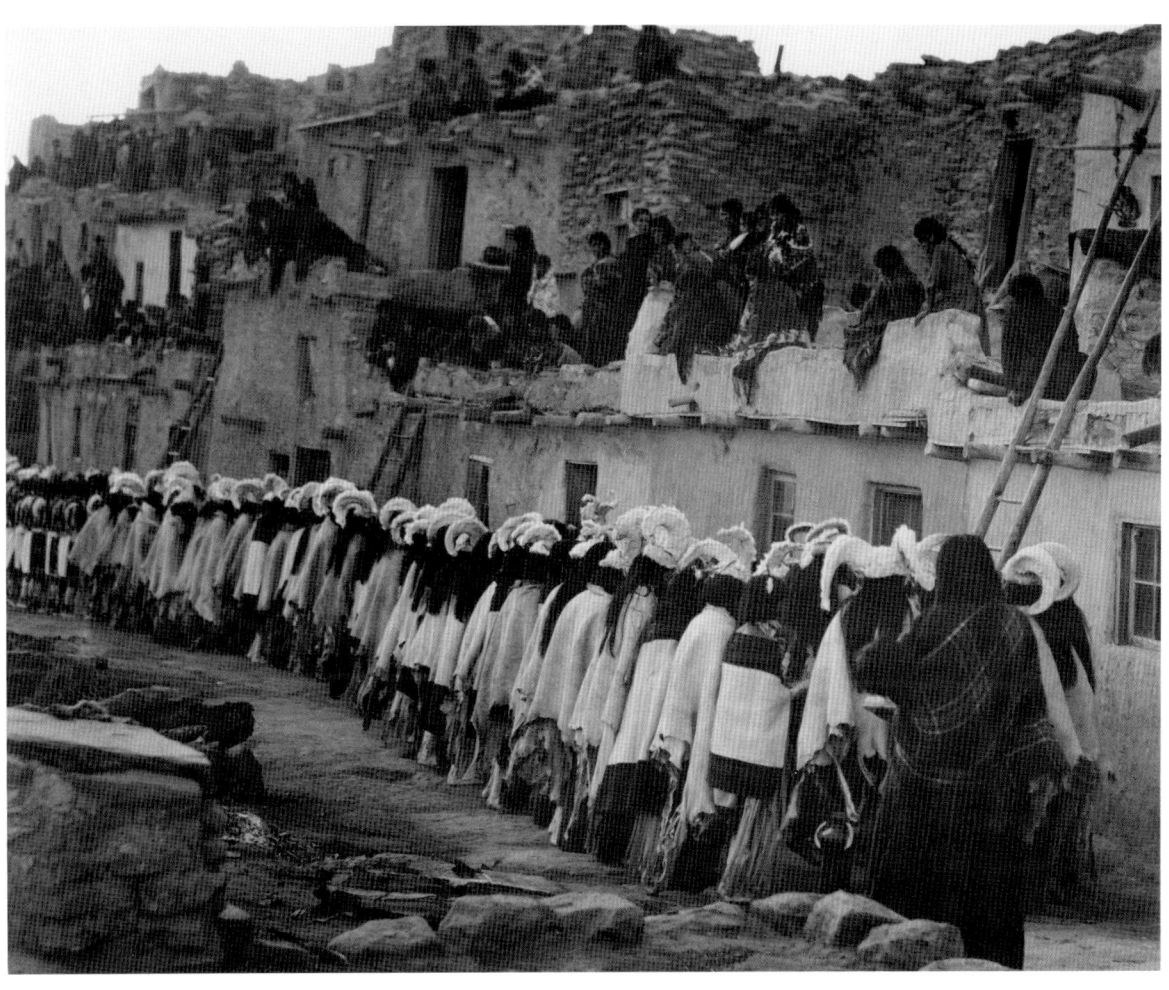

ACKNOWLEDGMENTS

WE OFFER GRATEFUL ACKNOWLEDGMENT TO THE MUSEUM OF Northern Arizona and to many members of the Museum staff. Katharine Bartlett's thorough knowledge of Hopi literature was indispensable. Hermann K. Bleibtreu lent his support and enthusiasm. Mark Middleton spent many painstaking hours assisting in the spotting of the reproduction prints.

In Flagstaff, Margaret Wright aided Barton Wright in his research and documentation of the Kate Cory images and the article A HOPI ESSAY. Attorney C. Benson Hufford researched and documented the status of the Kate Cory archive. David P. Seaman reviewed the linguistic diary of Kate Cory and evaluated the importance of her early linguistic observations. Linda Andrews provided helpful production advice.

In piecing together the details of Kate Cory's life, especially her years in Prescott, we relied on the kind help of the following people: Mr. and Mrs. Paul Rosenberger, Frank Guertan, Mr. and Mrs. Gail Gardner, Budge Ruffner, Mr. and Mrs. Charles Franklin Parker, Mrs. D. Sharp, and Bess Hoffman. We also thank the First Congregational Church of Prescott, Arizona, for the generous loan of the portrait of Kate Cory at the beginning of this book.

In addition, we offer special thanks to Charles and Dee March. And thanks to the Smoki Museum for their participation in this project.

Ansel and Virginia Adams and Laura Gilpin examined the Kate Cory images and provided us with artistic guidance. Their inspiration and enthusiasm encouraged us to proceed with publication.

We'd like to thank all those at Fabe Lithography, especially Stanley G. Fabe, photolithographer Mickey Delfiner and first pressman Skip Bogel.

Finally, we express particular gratitude to Mr. and Mrs. E. Cardon Walker and Mr. and Mrs. Peter G. Wray for their generosity. Their private funding enabled us to have the time and materials for the preparation of this book.

BIBLIOGRAPHY

Beaglehole, Ernest and Pearl.
Hopi of the Second Mesa. American Anthropological Association Memoir Number 44. Menasha. 1935.

Belknap, Bill.
Fred Kabotie: Hopi Indian Artist. Museum of Northern Arizona with Northland Press. Flagstaff. 1977.

Bradfield, Richard Maitland.
A Natural History of Associations: A Study in the Meaning of Community. Gerald Duckworth & Co., Ltd. London. 1973.

Bunzel, Ruth.
Zuni Kachinas. Forty-seventh Annual Report of the Bureau of American Ethnology. Washington. 1929-30.

Cory, Kate.
Personal Diary. (unpublished) Page 9. 1907.

Coze, Paul.
Introduction to the Hopi. Arizona Highways, Vol. XLVII. No. 6. Phoenix. 1971.

Crane, Leo.
Indians of the Enchanted Desert. Little, Brown, and Company. Boston. 1925.

Dockstader, Frederick J.
The Kachina and the White Man. Cranbrook Institute of Science, Bul. 35. Bloomfield Hills, Michigan. 1954.

Dozier, Edward P.
Hano, A Tewa Community in Arizona. Holt, Rinehart and Winston. New York. 1966.

Earle, Edwin and Kennard.
Hopi Kachinas. J.J. Augustin. New York. 1938.

Fewkes, Jesse Walter.
A Few Summer Ceremonials at the Tusayan Pueblos. A Journal of American Ethnology and Archaeology. Vol. 2. Houghton, Miflin & Co. Boston and New York. 1892.

The Group of Tusayan Ceremonials Called Katchinas. Bureau of American Ethnology, 15th. Annual Report. Washington. 1897.

Hopi Basket Dances. Journal of American Folklore. Vol. 12. No. 45. New York. 1899.

The New-Fire Ceremony at Walpi. American Anthropologist. New Series, Vol. II. No. 1. 1900.

Minor Hopi Festivals. American Anthropologist n.s., Vol. 4, New York. 1902.

Hopi Katchinas Drawn by Native Artists. Bureau of American Ethnology, 21st Annual Report. Washington. 1903.

Fewkes, Jesse Walter and Alexander M. Stephen.
The Na-ac-nai-ya: A Tusayan Initiation Ceremony. Journal of American Folklore, Vol. 5, No. 18. Boston. 1892.

Fewkes, Jesse Walter, assisted by Alexander M. Stephen and J.G. Owens.
The Snake Ceremonials at Walpi. A Journal of American Ethnology and Archaeology. Vol. 4. Houghton, Miflin & Co. Boston and New York. 1894.

Forde, Daryll C.
Hopi Agriculture and Land Ownership. Journal of the Royal Anthropological Institute, Vol. 61. London. 1931.

Garces, Father Francisco.
: *On the Trail of a Spanish Pioneer, the Diary and Itinerary of Francisco Garces—1776.* Vol. 1 and 2. Elliott Coues, Ed. Francis P. Harper. New York. 1900.

Hodge, Gene Meany.
: *The Kachinas are Coming.* Steller-Millar. Los Angeles. 1936.

Hough, Walter.
: *The Hopi Indians.* Torch Press. Cedar Rapids. 1915.

O'Kane, Walter Collins.
: *Sun in the Sky.* University of Oklahoma Press. Norman, Oklahoma. 1950.

Owens, J.G.
: *Natal Ceremonies of the Hopi Indians.* A Journal of American Ethnology and Archaeology, Vol. 2. Houghton, Miflin and Co. Boston and New York. 1892.

Parsons, Elsie Clews.
: *Pueblo Indian Journal 1920-1921, Introduction and Notes.* Memoirs of the American Anthropological Association, No. 32. New York. 1925.

: *Pueblo Indian Religion.* Chicago. 1939.

Simmons, Leo.
: *Sun Chief, Autobiography of a Hopi Indian.* Yale University Press. New Haven. 1942.

Stephen, Alexander M.
: *Hopi Journal of Alexander M. Stephen.* 2 Volumes. Edited by Elsie Clews Parsons. Columbus University Contributions to Anthropology, Vol. 23. New York. 1936.

Steward, Julian H.
: *Notes on Hopi Ceremonies in Their Initiatory Form in 1927-1928.* American Anthropological Association, Vol. 33, n.s. No. 1. New York. 1931.

Titiev, Mischa.
: *Old Orabi, A Study of the Hopi Indians of Third Mesa.* Papers of the Peabody Museum of American Archaeology and Ethnology, Vol. 22, No. 1. Harvard University. Cambridge. 1944.

Udall, Louise.
: *Me and Mine; The Life Story of Helen Sekaquaptewa.* University of Arizona Press. Tucson. 1969.

Underhill, Ruth.
: *First Penthouse Dwellers of America.* J.J. Augustin. New York. 1938.

Waters, Frank.
: *Masked Gods: Navaho & Pueblo Ceremonialism.* Swallow Press. Athens, Ohio. 1950.

Yamada, George.
: *The Great Resistance, A Hopi Anthology.* Published by the author. New York. 1957.

Yava, Albert.
: *Big Falling Snow.* University of New Mexico. Albuquerque. 1978.

This book was edited and designed by Bill Vaughn,
and typeset in Sabon and Gill Sans by Kitty Herrin.
Arrow Graphics & Typography, Missoula, Montana.